THE **NEAL-SCHUMAN** INDEX TO

FINGER-PLAYS

COMPILED BY KAY COOPER

NEAL-SCHUMAN INDEX SERIES
JIM ROGINSKI, SERIES EDITOR

NEAL-SCHUMAN PUBLISHERS, INC

NEW YORK   LONDON

Published by Neal-Schuman Publishers, Inc.
100 Varick Street
New York, NY 10013

Copyright ©1993 by Jim Roginski

Printed and bound in the United States of America

Library of Congress Cataloging-in-Publication Data

Cooper, Kay.
    Neal-Schuman index to fingerplays / compiled by Kay Cooper :
edited by Jim Roginski.
        p.   cm.– (Neal-Schuman indexes series : 4)
    Includes bibliographical references.
    ISBN 1-55570-149-3
    1. Finger play--Indexes. 2. Rhyming games--Indexes.
I. Roginski, James W., 1945-1993. II. Neal-Schuman Publishers.
III. Title. IV. Series.
GV1218.F5C65   1993
793.9--dc20   93-40099
                                                          CIP

For Ralph "Red" Camp, whose daughter, Karen,
teaches kindergarten.

Table of Contents

INTRODUCTION

Neal-Schuman Index to Fingerplays is a collection for pre-school, kindergarten, and elementary schoolteachers as well as for day-care people, Sunday school teachers, and librarians who work with children. In this book are two subject indexes, largely developed to supplement school curricula for lower elementary children. These indexes include fingerplays that help explain colors, numbers, the telling of time, cardinal directions, and abstract concepts, such as "up and down" and "narrow and wide." Religious rhymes as well as fingerplays appropriate for 17 holidays and the four seasons also are listed in the subject indexes.

Two special sections, designed especially for teachers, are *Fingerplays for Calendar Days* and *Fingerplays for Letter Days*. *Fingerplays for Calendar Days* lists rhymes to celebrate special days and events throughout the school year. By using the calendar, teachers can easily implement fingerplays into their classroom schedules. In the Fall, for example, are fingerplays appropriate for going back to school and safety rules, such as how to cross a street. Teachers also will find fingerplays that warn children to beware of strangers and one that explains to children what to do if their clothes catch on fire. Included in the *Calendar* are special days that every child will enjoy celebrating--Hat Day, Pooh Day, and Pancake Day. Many of these fingerplays may be used a couple of weeks before the events and enjoyed each day and even after the events have passed.

Fingerplays for Letter Days is designed for teachers who assign alphabet letters to days of the year. Fingerplays for the letter A, for example, include those about airplanes, alligators, ants, apples, acorns, and astronauts. Even the concept of "alone" is introduced.

If you are teaching a second or third language in school, you will enjoy the Language Rhyme section in the *Index by Subject* which lists fingerplays in 11 different languages. Fingerplays from 25 countries are also included and "World Hello Day" in *Fingerplays for Calendar Days* allows you to teach children how to say "hello" in five different languages.

Among the skills benefitted from using the fingerplays listed in this index are: artistic skills, body coordinations skills, classification skills, color recognition, counting skills, following directions skills, foreign language skills, health and safety skills, musical skills, natural science skills, pronunciation and spelling skills, rhythm and rhyming skills, role invention skills, self-awareness, size and shape recognition, tasting and smelling skills, and word recognition.

HOW TO USE THIS BOOK

Over 1600 fingerplays are listed alphabetically by first lines in the Main Index. When first line variations occur, the line most commonly used was selected for listing. A slash in the first line is for clarity of reading. Listings with identical or similar first lines have second lines.

Below each first line, sources for the play are listed in the left-hand column. All sources have three letter codes. Full bibliographical information for these codes is listed in the Bibliography. The right-hand column lists appropriate subjects for the fingerplay. In the columns, the following symbols are used:

(m)indicates music is given for the fingerplay

*marks the source that includes a fingerplay in a foreign language. When astericks are used, they also identify the foreign language in the subject column and the foreign language translation of the first line.

Following the Bibliography are two subject indexes: the Index by Subject and the Alphabetical by Subject Index. If you are searching for Halloween fingerplays, for example, you can find it listed under "Holidays" in the Index by Subject, and under "Halloween" in the Alphabetical by Subject Index. Following each entry is a set of numbers, which refer to fingerplays in the Main Index that cover Halloween. Plays are numerically listed.

In the Index by Subject are "additional" entries. For example, "Additional Birds" under the major subject category "Birds" lists fingerplays that are about "a bird" or a species included in one or two fingerplays.

In the Main Index and Alphabetical by Subject Index, "additional" entries are listed by their major subject names (usually in singular form), such as Bird, Food, Toy, and so forth.

Under the subject of Math, Countdown includes those fingerplays that present the process of counting backward from a starting number, such as five. Counting presents the process of counting forward and/or the introduction of a single number. Counting Out presents the process of counting to an arbitrary number until a player is "chosen."

Included in the back of this book are two special sections: Fingerplays for Calendar Days, which lists fingerplays to celebrate special days and events throughout the school year; and Fingerplays for Letter Days, which is for teachers who assign alphabet letters to days of the year.

PART
I

INDEX TO
FINGERPLAYS

A
_____

1. After my bath, I try, try, try to wipe myself 'til I'm dry, dry, dry

   FFR, RRR   Cleanliness

2. The airplane has great big wings

   ECT, FFr, RFF,   Airplane
   RRR   Up and Down

3. All around the cobbler's bench the monkey chased the weasel

   EWT (m), TLB   Animal, Monkey
                                    Cobbler
                                    Money

4. All do as I do

   RRR   Copy Cat Rhyme

5. All the children laughing, having lots of fun,/ playing tag and racing/ in
   the summer sun

   ECT   Safety Rule
                                    Sports or Hobbies

6. The alligator likes to swim

   LDF   Alligator or Crocodile

7. And one and two

   GFH   Counting

8. Anton, Anton, Anton Firulero, each one, each one, will play his own
   way, oh

   UBC (m)   Copy Cat Rhyme
                                    Costa Rica
                                    Musical Instrument

9. The ants go marching one by one, Hurrah, Hurrah

   DEH (m), TOB (m)   Ant
                                    Counting

3

Index to Fingerplays

10. Apple green, apple red

    ECT   Color
                                           Fruit

11. Are you sleeping, are you sleeping, Brother John *(Frere Jacques, Frere
    Jacques, Dormez-vous? Dormez-vous?)

    *ADR, *EmC,   Bell
    *TLB (m)   *French Language Rhyme
                                           Hand Rhyme

12. Around and about, around and about, over and under

    LiB, RRR   In and Out, Up and Down

13. As little Jenny Wren was sitting by the shed

    CCO, RRR   Mother Goose Rhyme
                                           Wren

14. Astronauts blast off in rockets 'way up into space

    FiO   Astronaut
                                           Night Sky
                                           Rocket Ship

15. At night I see the twinkling stars

    ECT, FiO, FoD,   Bedtime Rhyme
    RRR, TCB   Night Sky

16. At the curb before I cross, I stop my running feet

    FFr   Left and Right
                                           Safety Rule
                                           Senses

17. At the zoo we saw a bear

    MiM   Bear, Elephant, Giraffe,
                                             Lion, Monkey

18. The attendant puts gas into our car

    ECT   Car
                                           Career

19. Attention, attention, Company A: My fingers are playing soldier today

      FFr, RFF   Counting
                                               Left and Right
                                               Soldier

20. Auto, auto, may I have a ride

      LDF, RRR   Car

21. The autumn leaves come dancing down

      FPF   Color
                                             Fall
                                             Quiet Time Rhyme
                                             Tree

22. The autumn leaves have fallen down

      GaY   Chores
                                             Fall
                                             Tree
                                             Wind

23. Away up high in the apple tree, two red apples smiled at me

      FFr, FiO, RFF,   Apple Tree
      RRR   Counting
                                             Fall
                                           Fruit
                                           Up and Down

B

24. Baby, baby, little as can be *(Bimbo, bimbo, piccolino)

      *RFF   Baby
                                             Counting
                                         Finger Rhyme
                                           *Italian Language Rhyme
                                           Left and Right

Index to Fingerplays

34. The bass viol is big and tall

      FuG   Musical Instrument
                                                 Size

35. The bear went over the mountain

      EWT (m), LDF, PBS,   Bear
      TOB (m), TPM   Mountain

36. Bears, bears, bears everywhere

      ECT, PRh, RRR   Teddy Bear

37. Beat, beat with your feet,/ we're playing the body band

      ECT   Animal Sounds
                                                 Musical Instrument
                                                 Senses

38. Bee, bee, bumblebee

      LDF   Bee
                                                     Counting Out
                                                 Pig

39. Before I jump into my bed

      RRR   Bedtime Rhyme
                                                       Shoes and Boots

40. Before Noah's big, big boat started on that long, long float

      RRR   Bird
                                                        Boat
                                                 Religious Rhyme
                                                 Size

41. Bend and stretch, reach for the stars

      RRR   Night Sky

42. The Bible is God's Word

      LAL   Religious Rhyme

43. A big black cat with eyes so green went out on the night of Halloween

      FFr   Cat
                                           Halloween

53. Boom, boom! Beat the drum

      FFr, GFH
                             Fourth of July
                             Musical Instrument
                             United States

54. Boom! Boom! Boom! Goes the big brass drum

      ECT, RRR, TCB
                         Fourth of July
                         Musical Instrument
                         Size
                         United States

55. Boots never seem to fit

      FFr
                         Shoes and Boots
                         Size

56. Bounce and catch it

      RFF
                         Ball
                         Game

57. Bow, bow, bow Belinda

      DEH (m)
                         Following Commands
                         Left and Right

58. The brave little hunter went hunting for a bear

      RRR, TCB, WDS
                         Bear
                         Hunting

59. Bread in Mexico is round and flat

      MUD
                         Bread
                         France, India, Israel,
                            Mexico
                         Friendship
                         Shape

60. Bright colored bumble bee

      ECT
                         Bee

61. Bright colored butterfly

      FFr
                         Butterfly and Caterpillar

Index to Fingerplays

62. Brother, come and dance with me

EWT (m)

Counting
Left and Right
Senses
Sports or Hobbies

63. Brow brinky

TeF

Touching Rhyme

64. The brown kangaroo is very funny

FFr

Kangaroo

65. The brushes in my home are simply everywhere

ECT

Chores
Health

66. Build a house with five bricks

GaY

Counting
Store or Building
Wind

67. "The bunnies now must go to bed," the furry mother bunny said

CCO

Bedtime Rhyme
Counting
Rabbit

68. Busy little finger people, who will put the toys away

CCO

Chores
Counting
Helping Others

69. The busy windshield wiper goes "A-dash, a-dash, a-dash"

SAP

Car
Rain

70. Bye, baby bunting, Daddy's gone a hunting/ to get a little rabbit skin

DEH (m), MuF (m)

Baby, Family
Hunting
Mother Goose Rhyme
Rabbit

71. Bye, baby bunting, Father's gone a hunting; Mother's gone a'milking

        CCO

                                        Baby, Family
                                        Counting
                                        Hunting
                                        Mother Goose Rhyme

C

72. C—that's the way it begins

        MuG (m)

                                        Chicken
                                        Pat-a-Cake Rhyme
                                        Spelling Rhyme

73. Call the puppy, give him some milk

        ECT, RRR

                                        Chores
                                        Dog
                                        Helping Others

74. Can you be a carpenter

        RRR

                                        Carpenter
                                        Size
                                        Tool

75. Can you hop like a rabbit

        ECT, PRh, RRR

                                        Bird, Duck
                                      Copy Cat Rhyme
                                      Dog, Fish, Frog or Toad,
                                           Rabbit
                                      Quiet Time Rhyme

76. Can you plant a cabbage, dear

        DEH (m)

                                        Plants and Seeds
                                        Vegetable

Index to Fingerplays

84. Children can hop on one leg

      TPM   Cat
                                   Counting
                                   Nature

85. Children put your pants on

      LDF   Clothes
                                   Counting
                                   Dressing

86. The children ran to see Jesus one day

      FPF   Religious Rhyme

87. Chip-chop, chip-chop, Chipper, Chopper Joe

      GaY   Career

88. Choo, choo, choo, the train runs down the track

      FPF, LDF   Train

89. Chop, chop, choppity-chop

      ADR, GaY   Vegetable

90. Christmas is a-coming, the geese are getting fat

      LDF   Christmas
                                   Goose
                                   Money
                                   Mother Goose Rhyme

91. Christmas is a happy time. It's time for bells to chime

      CCO   Bell
                                   Christmas
                                   Counting
                                   Feelings

92. Christmas is a happy time. It's time to sing

      LAL   Christmas, Easter
                                   Feelings
                                   Religious Rhyme

Index to Fingerplays

100. Clap your hands, clap your hands, clap them just like me

      FiR, JTJ, LDF,   Copy Cat Rhyme
      PBS   Hand Rhyme
                               Quiet Time Rhyme
                               Touching Rhyme

101. Clap your hands, 1, 2, 3

      RRR   Copy Cat Rhyme
                               Counting
                               Hand Rhyme

102. Clap your hands so gaily

      RRR   Counting
                               Hand Rhyme

103. Click-Clack, click-clack, back and forth

      FFr   Back and Forth
                               Car

104. Climb the ladder and down we slide

      RFF, RRR   Playground
                               Up and Down

105. Climb up the ladder, hang on to the side

      RRR   Playground
                               Safety Rule
                               Up and Down

106. Climbing, climbing up the ladder

      RRR   Playground
                               Sharing
                               Up and Down

107. Climbing, climbing up the stairs

      FFr   Bedtime Rhyme
                               Cleanliness
                               Religious Rhyme

Index to Fingerplays

116. Come follow, follow, follow

  LDF   Touching Rhyme

117. "Come, little children," calls mother hen

  RRR   Bedtime Rhyme
                                    Chicken

118. "Come my bunnies, it's time for bed"

  FFr, RRR   Bedtime Rhyme
                                    Counting
                                    Rabbit

119. Come see my small garden, how sweetly they grow

  CCO   Counting
                                    Flower, Rose
                                    Helping Others
                                    Plants and Seeds
                                    Size
                                    Sun

120. Come to the store with me

  LiB, RRR   Bread, Dessert, Food, Fruit
                                    Family
                                    Store or Building

121. Corn grows tall, pumpkins crawl

  MUD   Apple Tree
                                    Fruit, Vegetable
                                    Plants and Seeds
                                    Up and Down

122. Creep, little mousie, come along to me

  GaY   Cat, Mouse

123. Creeping, creeping, creeping, comes the little cat

  FFr, HRh, RRR   Cat, Rabbit

124. Creeping, creeping to my head

  CCO   Bedtime Rhyme

D

132. Dewey was a captain at Manila Bay

      DEH (m)

                        Feelings
                        Months and Days
                        Philippines
                        Sea and Seashore

133. Did you ever see a noodlehead

      MUD

                        Copy Cat Rhyme
                        Food

134. Dig a little hole

      FPF, LiB, RRR,
      TCB

                        Plants and Seeds
                        Rose
                        Sun

135. Dig! Dig! Dig! Rake just so

      RRR

                        Plants and Seeds
                        Rain, Sun

136. The digger goes up

      SAP

                        Machine
                        Up and Down

137. Dirt comes in colors, black, red, and brown

      ECT

                        Animal Home
                        Color
                        Nature

138. Dirty hands are such a fright

      FFr

                        Cleanliness

139. The dishes need washing

      ECT, TCB

                        Chores
                        Family
                        Helping Others
                        Kitchen Utensils or Dishes

140. Dive, little tadpole, one

      FFr, RFF

                        Counting
                        Frog or Toad

Index to Fingerplays

150. Down the chimney dear Santa Claus crept

      FPF, LDF   Christmas
                                            Counting
                                            Santa Claus

151. Down the street I'm hurrying

      SAP   Mail
                                              Mail Carrier
                                            Months and Days
                                            Valentine's Day

152. Draw a circle, draw a circle, made very round

      ECT   Shape

153. Draw a circle, draw a circle, round as can be

      FFr, RFF, RRR   Shape

154. Draw a square

      ECT, FFr, RFF, RRR   Shape

155. Draw a triangle

      ECT, FFr, RFF, RRR   Shape

156. Dreidel, dreidel, dreidel—see the spinning top

      MiM   Color
                                            Countdown
                                          Hanukkah
                                          Religious Rhyme

157. Drip, drop, drip, spring rain has come no doubt

      FPF   Rain
                                              Spring

158. Dry dirt, wet dirt, oh, what fun

      ECT   Nature
                                              Opposites

E

159. An eagle dives and glides

    MyB   Bird
                                         Monkey, Snake

160. The earth is a great big ball

    CCO, FiO   Earth and Sky
                                         Shape

161. Earth is round

    CCO   Earth and Sky
                                       Shape

162. Easter bunny hop hop hop

    BPP   Easter
                                       Rabbit (Easter)

163. Easter bunny hops along

    CCO   Color
                                     Easter
                                     Rabbit (Easter)

164. Easter Bunny's ears are floppy

    RRR, TCB   Easter
                                     Rabbit (Easter)

165. Easter duck and Easter chick

    CCO   Easter
                                     Feelings
                                   Food
                                   Hat
                                   Rabbit (Easter)

166. Easter eggs here

    FPF   Easter
                                     Eggs
                                   Hiding

167. Easter is a happy time

    FFu, RRR

Bell
Easter
Feelings
Flower
Religious Rhyme
Store or Building

168. The Easter rabbit came one day

    CCO

Easter
Rabbit (Easter)
Up and Down

169. The Easter Rabbit's helpers, five in a row

    CCO

Counting
Easter
Rabbit (Easter)

170. Eeny, meeny, miney, mo

    LDF, SaG (m)

Counting Out

171. An eency weency spider went up the waterspout

ADR, BFG, CCO,
EWT (m), FFr,
FFu, FiR, FPF,
GaY, GDW (m),
GFH, JTJ, LDF,
MuF (m), PAT, PBS,
ReG, RFF, RRR,
SaG (m), TeF,
TNT, TOB (m), TPM,
WAA (m)

Rain, Sun
Spider
Structure
Up and Down

172. Eight little candles in a row waiting to join the holiday glow. The first night we light candle number one

    SmC

Candle
Counting
Hanukkah
Religious Rhyme

173. 8 little candles in a row waiting to join the holiday glow. We will light
these one by one

        SmC   Candle
                                                 Counting
    Hanukkah
    Religious Rhyme

174. Eight tiny reindeer pawing in the snow

    FFr, RFF   Christmas
    Counting
    Reindeer (Santa's)
    Santa Claus

175. An elephant goes like this and that

    ADR, BPP, GaY,   Elephant
    GFH, PBS, TNT   Size

176. The elephant has a great big trunk

    FFr   Elephant
    Size
    Up and Down

177. The elephant has a trunk for a nose

    FFr, RFF   Elephant
    Size
    Up and Down

178. Elm trees stretch and stretch so wide

    ECT, RRR, TCB   Concept, Size
    Tree

179. Every day when we eat our dinner our table is very small

    BPP, FFr, FFu,   Counting
    FiO, LDF, RFF,   Family
    RRR   Size
    Structure
    Thanksgiving

180. Every morning at half-past eight I go oo-oo-oo-oo-ooh to Georgie

    DEH (m)   Telling Time

181. Eye winker, Tom Tinker

      EWT (m), FP2   Senses
      LDF, RRR, TLB (m)   Tickling Rhyme
                                Touching Rhyme

182. Eyes to see with

      ECT, RRR   Senses
                                Touching Rhyme

183. Eyes up * (Agari me)

      *TLB (m)   *Japanese Language Rhyme
                                Senses
                                Shape
                                Up and Down

F

---

184. A face so round and eyes so bright

      RRR   Guessing Rhyme
                                Halloween
                                Jack-o-Lantern
                                Touching Rhyme

185. A family of rabbits lived under a tree

      FFr, RFF   Addition, Counting
                                Animal Home
                                Day and Night, Up
                                    and Down
                                Rabbit

186. "The farmer and the miller have worked," the mother said

      FiN (m)   Bread

187. The farmer plants the seeds

      RRR   Bread
                                Farmer
                                Plants and Seeds
                                Rain, Sun

Index to Fingerplays

188. The farmer wakes up early and puts on his workday clothes

   SAP

   Chicken
   Cow
   Farmer

189. A fat bunny rabbit with ears so tall

   RRR, TCB

   Rabbit

190. A father and mother bird lived in a tree

   RRR

   Animal Home
   Bird
   Cat
   Counting
   Spring
   Tree

191. Fee, fie, fo, fum, see my finger

   LDF, RRR

   Finger Rhyme
   Hiding

192. A fence is tall

   FiO

   Size
   Structure

193. The ferris wheel goes up so high

   ECT

   Circus or Carnival
   Machine
   Up and Down

194. The fiddle sings twiddle, dee, dee

   FuG

   Musical Instrument

195. The Finger Band is coming to town

   GFH, LDF, RRR,
   TCB

   Flag
   Finger Rhyme
   Hat
   Musical Instrument

196. Fingers, fingers, everywhere

   RRR

   Finger Rhyme

26

197. Fingers, fingers, flit and fly

      MyB   Finger Rhyme
                                    Quiet Time Rhyme

198. Fingers like to wiggle, waggle

      GaY   Finger Rhyme

199. The fire station's empty

      ECT   Fire Fighter
                                    Store or Building

200. Fireworks bursting in the night

      SmC   Bastille Day
                                    Countdown
                                    France

201. First, a little nest in an apple tree

      RRR   Animal Home
                                    Animal Sounds
                                    Apple Tree
                                    Counting
                                    Robin
                                    Spring, Summer

202. First grade babies

      TOB (m)   Addition, Counting

203. First I loosen the mud and dirt

      ECT, LDF, RRR   Cleanliness
                                    Shoes and Boots

204. The first little clown is fat and gay

      MiM   Clown
                                    Counting
                                    Size

205. The first little pig danced a merry, merry jig

      CCO   Counting
                                    Pig

Index to Fingerplays

206. First the body and then the head

      LiB, RRR
                              Snowman
                              Winter

207. First the farmer plows the ground

      RRR
                              Farmer
                              Plants and Seeds
                              Rain, Sun
                              Vegetable

208. First the farmer sows his seeds

      CCO
                              Farmer
                              Plants and Seeds

209. First you push him out of sight

      CCO
                              Jack-in-the-Box

210. First you take a pumpkin

      FFr
                                Halloween
                              Jack-o-Lantern

211. The fish lives in the brook

      CCO, FiO, LDF
                              Animal Home
                              Bird
                              Fish
                              Store or Building
                              Water Bodies

212. Five at the table sitting by the door

      FPF
                              Countdown
                              Structure

213. Five big turkeys sitting on the gate

      BPP, MiM
                              Animal Sounds
                              Counting
                              Hiding
                              Thanksgiving
                              Turkey

214. Five birthday candles. Wish there were more

      LiA, PBS

                    Birthday
                    Candle
                    Countdown

215. Five black cats sat on a fence

      LiA

                    Cat
                    Counting
                    Halloween
                    Spelling Rhyme
                    Witch

216. Five bright stars on Christmas night wanted to give their very brightest light

      MiM, RFF

                    Christmas
                    Counting
                    Night Sky
                    Religious Rhyme

217. Five brown pennies in my purse

      FPH, RFF, RRR,
      TCB

                    Birthday
                    Counting
                    Money

218. Five brown teddies sitting on a wall

      TNT

                    Countdown
                    Teddy Bear

219. Five candles on a birthday cake

      MiM

                    Birthday
                    Candle
                    Countdown
                    Dessert

220. Five cheerful valentines from the ten-cent store

      MiM

                    Countdown
                    Valentine's Day
                    Store or Building

Index to Fingerplays

221. Five children dreamed of Christmas day
        RFF
                                    Bedtime Rhyme
                                    Christmas
                                    Counting

222. Five Christmas trees in a forest green
        MiM
                                    Christmas
                                    Christmas Tree
                                    Counting

223. Five circus ponies all in a row
        MiM
                                    Circus or Carnival
                                    Countdown
                                    Horse

224. Five currant buns in a baker's shop
        GaY, Sta
                                    .Bread
                                    Countdown
                                    Money
                                    Store or Building

225. Five Easter rabbits standing by the door
        MiM
                                    Countdown
                                    Easter
                                    Rabbit (Easter)

226. Five eggs and five eggs, that makes ten
        ECT, RFF, RRR
                                    Addition
                                    Animal Sounds
                                    Chicken
                                    Eggs

227. Five enormous dinosaurs letting out a roar
        MiM
                                    Animal Sounds
                                    Countdown
                                    Dinosaur

228. Five fat turkeys all gobbling about
        FPH
                                    Counting
                                    Thanksgiving
                                    Turkey

229. Five fat turkeys are we

       BBP, FFr

Animal Sounds
Counting
Thanksgiving
Turkey

230. Five fat turkeys were sitting on a fence

       FFr

Counting
Thanksgiving
Turkey

231. Five fingers on this hand

       ECT, LDF, RRR,
       TLB (m)

Baby
Counting
Growing Up
Touching Rhyme

232. Five, four, three, two, one, zero

       FPF

Astronaut
Countdown
Left and Right
Rocket Ship

233. Five gay valentines from the ten-cent store

       FFr, RFF, RRR

Color
Countdown
Family
Store or Building
Valentine's Day

234. Five gray elephants marching through a glade

       FFr

Animal Sounds
Counting
Elephant

241. Five little birds without any home

   FFr, RRR

   Animal Home
   Bird
   Counting
   Tree

242. Five little bunnies hopping down the road

   FPH

   Counting
   Easter
   Rabbit (Easter)
   Spring

243. Five little bunnies in a bakery shop

   BPP, CCO,
   MiM

   Countdown
   Dessert
   Money
   Store or Building

244. Five little busy bees on a day so sunny

   FFr, RFF

   Animal Sounds
   Bee
   Counting

245. Five little chickadees sitting at the door

   CCO, FFr, FPF,
   LDF, MiM, RRR,
   SDG (m)

   Chickadee
   Countdown

246. Five little chickens by the old barn door

   RFF

   Chicken
   Countdown
   Insect

247. Five little children on Thanksgiving Day

   MiM

   Counting
   Food
   Religious Rhyme
   Thanksgiving

255. Five little Easter eggs lovely colors wore

        FFr, FiO, RFF,   Color
        RRR   Countdown
                                 Easter
                                 Eggs
                                 Family

256. Five little Easter rabbits sitting by the door

        FFr, RFF   Countdown
                                 Easter
                                 Rabbit (Easter)

257. Five little elephants rowing toward the shore

        ECT, RRR   Countdown
                                 Elephant

258. Five little farmers woke up with the sun

        CCO, ECT, RRR   Chores
                                 Counting
                                 Farmer
                                 Machine

259. Five little firefighters sit very still

        FFr, MiM, RFF,   Counting
        RRR   Fire Engine
                                 Fire Fighter

260. Five little fishes swimming in a pool

        MiM   Boat
                                 Counting
                                 Fish
                                 Water Bodies

261. Five little fishes were swimming near the shore

        RRR   Countdown
                                 Fish
                                 Sea and Seashore

269. Five little ghosts went haunting on Halloween night

      FPH

                            Counting
                            Feelings
                            Ghost or Goblin
                            Halloween

270. Five little ghosts went out to play

      MiM

                            Countdown
                            Ghost or Goblin
                            Halloween

271. Five little girls woke up in their beds

      LDF, MiM

                            Counting
                            Dressing
                            Telling Time

272. Five little goblins on a Halloween night made a very, very spooky sight

      FFr, HRh, MiM,
      RFF, RRR

                            Counting
                            Ghost or Goblin
                            Halloween

273. Five little ground hogs one February day crept out of their dens

      FPH

                            Animal
                            Animal Home, Shadow
                            Counting
                            Ground-hog Day
                            Months and Days

274. Five little hearts all in a row

      FPH

                            Counting
                            Feelings
                            Friendship
                            Valentine's Day

275. Five little hunters looking for deer

      RRR

                            Animal, Bear
                            Counting
                            Hunting

Index to Fingerplays

276. Five little Indians by the tipi door

    FPH   Countdown
                                            Indian

277. Five little Indians on a nice fall day jumped on their ponies and rode far away

    FoD   Counting
                                            Horse
                                          Indian

278. Five little Indians running through a door

    LDF   Countdown
                                            Indian

279. Five little Irishmen all looking for a four-leaf clover

    FPH   Counting
                                            Ireland
                                          Plants and Seeds
                                          St. Patrick's Day

280. Five little jack-o-lanterns sitting on a gate

    BPP, CCO, FFr,   Counting
    FPF, GFH, LDF   Halloween
                                              Jack-o-Lantern

281. Five little jinny birds hopping by my door

    MiM   Countdown
                                            Wren

282. Five little kites flying high in the sky

    MiM   Counting
                                            Earth and Sky
                                          Kite

283. Five little kittens playing on the floor

    RFF   Cat
                                            Countdown

284. Five little kittens sleeping on a chair

HRh, RRR

Cat
Countdown

285. Five little kittens standing in a row

BPP, LDF, PBS

Animal Sounds
Cat, Dog
Counting
Left and Right

286. Five little ladies going for a walk

GaY

Addition
Sports or Hobbies

287. Five little leaves in the autumn breeze tumbled and fluttered from the trees

MiM

Color
Counting
Fall
Tree

288. Five little leaves so bright and gay were dancing about on a tree one day

GaY

Countdown
Fall
Tree
Wind

289. Five little letters lying on a tray

FFr

Countdown
Family
Feelings
Mail

290. Five little May baskets waiting by the door

FFr, RFF

Color
Countdown
Feelings
Friendship
May Day
Months and Days
Sharing

299. Five little peas in a pea-pod pressed

     ADR, GaY

                       Counting
                       Plants and Seeds
                       Vegetable

300. Five little pennies—I took to the store

     MiM

                       Countdown
                       Money
                       Store or Building

301. Five little pilgrims fish in the morn

     MUD

                       Addition, Counting
                       Bread, Food
                       Friendship
                       Indian
                       Pilgrim
                       Thanksgiving

302. Five little pilgrims on Thanksgiving Day

     CCO, FFr, RFF

                       Counting
                       Food
                       Pilgrim
                       Thanksgiving

303. Five little pigs out by the old farm gate

     FPH

                       Counting
                       Pig

304. Five little polar bears playing on the shore

     FFr

                       Bear
                       Countdown
                       Sea and Seashore

305. Five little ponies all dapple gray

     RRR

                       Animal Sounds
                       Counting
                       Horse

306. Five little pumpkins sitting by the door

        FPH   Countdown
                                       Fruit
                                       Halloween

307. Five little pumpkins sitting on a gate

        EWT (m), MiM,   Counting
        PBS, RRR, TCB   Fruit
                                       Halloween
                                       Wind

308. Five little pumpkins were standing in a row

        FoD   Counting
                                       Fruit
                                       Halloween

309. Five little puppies were playing in the sun

        PBS, RFF   Counting
                                       Dog

310. Five little puppy dogs in a kennel door

        RRR   Countdown
                                       Dog

311. Five little pussy cats playing near the door

        GaY   Cat
                                       Countdown

312. Five little pussy cats; see them play

        RFF   Animal Sounds
                                     Cat, Mouse
                                     Counting

313. Five little rabbits under a log

        FFr, RFF   Counting
                                     Feelings
                                     Hiding
                                     Rabbit
                                     Senses

314. Five little rag dolls sitting up tall

    FuG

    Counting
    Doll

315. Five little reindeer standing in a row

    CCO

    Christmas
    Counting
    Reindeer (Santa's)
    Santa Claus

316. Five little robins lived in a tree

    FFr, MiM, RFF,
    RRR

    Addition, Counting
    Robin

317. Five little sailors putting out to sea

    FFr, RFF

    Counting
    Sailor
    Size

318. Five little seashells lying on the shore

    FFr, MiM, RFF

    Countdown
    Sea and Seashore

319. Five little seeds a-sleeping they lay

    GaY

    Bird
    Countdown
    Plants and Seeds

320. Five little shamrocks lying in the grass

    MiM

    Countdown
    Fairy or Giant
    Plants and Seeds
    St. Patrick's Day

321. Five little snowmen, happy and gay

    FiO, FoD, RRR

    Counting
    Feelings
    Months and Days
    Snowman
    Spring, Winter

Index to Fingerplays

330. Five little squirrels sitting in a tree

      CCO, FFr, FFu,   Counting
      GFH, MiM, RFF   Hunting
                                    Squirrel

331. Five little teddy bears on my bedroom floor

      FPH   Bedtime Rhyme
                                    Countdown
                                    Teddy Bear

332. Five little tulips bright and gay

      FoD   Counting
                                    Day and Night, Open
                                      and Shut
                                    Flower
                                    Plants and Seeds
                                    Spring

333. Five little turkeys flew up in a tree

      FFr   Counting
                                    Thanksgiving
                                    Turkey

334. Five little turkeys standing in a row

      CCO   Counting
                                    Thanksgiving
                                    Turkey

335. Five little turkeys were standing by a door

      FiO, FoD   Countdown
                                    Thanksgiving
                                    Turkey

336. Five little valentines all in place

      FPF   Counting
                                    Valentine's Day

337. Five little valentines were having a race

      FFr, RRR, TCB   Counting
                                    Valentine's Day

Index to Fingerplays

346. Five red apples in a grocery store

     RFF   Countdown
                             Fall
                             Fruit
                             Store or Building

347. Five red stockings heard the fire roar

     MiM   Christmas
                             Clothes
                             Countdown
                             Feelings

348. Five timid pumpkins are marching in a row

     FFr   Countdown
                             Fruit
                             Halloween

349. Five wooden soldiers standing in a row

     FFr, RFF, RRR   Countdown
                             Toy Soldier

350. The flag is coming

     TCB   Flag
                             Fourth of July
                             Peace
                             United States

351. Flapjacks, flapjacks, hot-on-the-griddle cake

     MUD   Pancakes

352. Flop your arms

     RRR   Doll

353. The flower holds up its little cup

     RRR   Flower
                             Rain
                             Tree

Index to Fingerplays

354. Flowers are sweet

      RRR   Counting Out
                                      Valentine's Day

355. Flowers grow like this

      ADR, GaY   Growing Up
                                      Plants and Seeds
                                      Tree

356. Flowers tall, flowers small

      FFr, FiO, RFF   Counting
                                        Flower
                                      Size
                                      Spring

357. Four little boys sat on a bus

      WDS   Bus
                                        Counting
                                      Feelings

358. Four little candles all in a ring/ announcing the coming of our King

      SmC   Christmas
                                        Counting
                                      Religious Rhyme

359. Four little turkeys lived in a pen

      FiO   Counting
                                        Feelings
                                      Thanksgiving
                                      Turkey

360. Four scarlet berries left upon the tree

      GaY   Blackbird
                                        Counting
                                      Manners
                                      Tree

361. The Fourth of July! Oh, what a great day

      FPH   Counting
                                        Fourth of July
                                      United States

362. Fred had a fish bowl

        ECT, RFF, RRR   Addition, Counting
                                                Fish

363. Friendly ghosts are on their flight

        FPF   Ghost or Goblin
                                                Halloween
                                              Hiding

364. Friends, I have quite a few

        TCB   Counting Out
                                              Friendship
                                              Valentine's Day

365. From big black clouds the raindrops fell

        ECT, RRR   Earth and Sky
                                              Rain, Rainbow, Sun

366. The funny, fat walrus sits in the sea

        FFr   Animal
                                                Sea and Seashore

367. Fuzzy little caterpillar crawling, crawling on the ground

        FiN (m), FFr   Animal Home
                                            Butterfly and Caterpillar
                                            Fall, Spring

368. Fuzzy wuzzy caterpillar into a corner will creep

        ECT, RRR   Animal Home
                                            Butterfly and Caterpillar
                                            Fall, Spring

G

369. Gather snow and make a ball

        FFr   Snowman
                                                Winter

Index to Fingerplays

394. Gray squirrel, gray squirrel, swish your bushy tail

    ECT, RRR, TCB,   Squirrel
    TeF

395. A great big ball, a middle-sized ball, a little ball I see

    CCO, LDF   Ball
                                    Counting
                                    Size

396. The great big train goes up the track

    LDF   Train

397. Great Christmas bells sing Ding Dong Ding

    BPP   Bell
                                    Christmas
                                    Fast and Slow
                                    Size

398. Green, green, green, green

    TCB   Color
                                    St. Patrick's Day

399. Green Sally up, Green Sally down,/ Green Sally bake her
    possum brown

    StD (m)   Pat-a-Cake Rhyme

400. Grey smoke curling to the sky rises out of chimneys high

    SAP   Smoke

401. Guiseppi, the cobbler mends my shoes

    RRR   Cobbler
                                    Shoes and Boots
                                    Size

402. Gum drop, gum drop, in a bowl

    MUD   Counting
                                    Food
                                    Guessing Rhyme

H

410. Happy children in the springtime

    RRR

                             Copy Cat Rhyme
                             Fall, Spring, Summer,
                                Winter
                             Feelings

411. Hat on head, chin strap here,/ snap just so, you see

    RRR

                             Clothes, Hat, Mittens,
                                Shoes and Boots
                             Counting
                             Dressing

412. Have you seen the little ducks swimming in the water

    ADR, GaY   Duck

413. He looks to the left

    BPP

                             Animal Sounds
                             Left and Right
                             Owl

414. Head and shoulder, baby

    StD (m)

                             Ball
                             Counting
                             Cow
                             Pat-a-Cake Rhyme
                             Store or Building
                             Touching Rhyme

415. Head bumper, eye winker

    PAT, TTB

                             Tickling Rhyme
                             Touching Rhyme

416. Head, shoulders, knees, and toes *(Ulu, uauau, tulivae tamatamivae)

    ADR, DEH (m), ECT,   *Samoan Language Rhyme
    FPF, GaY, GFH,   Touching Rhyme
    MuG (m), PAT, RRR,
    *TLB (m), TNT

417. Hear the merry Christmas bells

    LDF

                             Bell
                             Christmas

Index to Fingerplays

418. Hello! Take off your hat

        DEH (m)

                                          Birthday
                                          Dessert, Food
                                          Cleanliness
                                          Clothes, Hat, Shoes and
                                              Boots

419. Help me wind my ball of wool

        GaY (m)   Craft

420. A hen sits on a wall *(Une poule sur un mur)

        *TLB (m)   Chicken
                                          *French Language Rhyme
                                        Tickling Rhyme

421. Here are balloons for a party, for it is my birthday today

        MiM   Balloon
                                          Birthday
                                          Countdown
                                          Color
                                          Sharing

422. Here are Bobby's new white shoes

        RRR   Helping Others
                                          Shoes and Boots

423. Here are Grandma's spectacles, and here is Grandma's cap

        ADR, CCO, EWT (m),   Grandparents
        FFr, FiO, FiR,   Hat
        FPF, FuG, GaY,
        LDF, ReG, RFF,
        RRR

424. Here are little Jim and Jane going for a walk

        CCO   Friendship
                                          Rain, Sun

425. Here are mother's knives and forks

      CCO, FFr, FFu,   Family
      FiO, FPF, FP2,   Kitchen Utensils or Dishes
      GaY, ReG, RFF,   Structure
      RRR, SaG (m),
      TeF, TNT, TPM

426. Here are my ears

      RRR   Senses
                                   Touching Rhyme

427. Here are my eyes, one and two

      ECT, RRR   Counting
                                   Day and Night
                                   Senses
                                   Touching Rhyme

428. Here are two apple buds growing on a tree

      ECT   Apple Tree
                                   Plants and Seeds
                                   Sun

429. Here are two telegraph poles

      CCO, FFr, LDF   Bird
                                   Counting
                                   Structure

430. Here comes a bunny, hippity-hoppity-hip

      FPF   Counting
                                   Rabbit
                                   Touching Rhyme

431. Here comes Jocko prancing

      SAP   Toy
                                   Up and Down

432. Here comes the choo choo train

      BPP   Back and Forth
                                   Train

441. Here is a chimney. Here is the top

      BPP, CCO, FiO,   Christmas
      FPF, GFH, LDF,   Santa Claus
      TCB

442. Here is a froggie, hippety-hop

      RFF   Frog or Toad

443. Here is a giant who is tall, tall, tall

      GFH, RFF   Fairy or Giant
                            Size

444. Here is a house built up high

      GaY, TLB (m)   Mouse
                            Store or Building

445. Here is a house for Jimmy

      RRR   Counting
                            Family
                            Feelings
                            Helping Others
                            Store or Building

446. Here is a house with two little people

      GaY   Cat
                            Counting
                            Store or Building

447. Here is a kitty

      FiO   Bedtime Rhyme
                            Cat, Rabbit
                            Friendship

448. Here is a little puppy

      LiA   Cat, Dog
                            Tickling Rhyme

Index to Fingerplays

456. Here is a window in a toy shop

      FFr, RFF, RRR

Balloon, Doll, Top, Toy
   Soldier
Store or Building

457. Here is a yellow daffodil

      FFr, FiO, RFF

Flower
Left and Right
Spring

458. Here is an engine

      RRR

Train

459. Here is an oak tree straight and tall

      ECT, RRR, TCB

Animal Home
Bird
Counting
Size
Tree

460. Here is baby's tousled head

      FFr, RFF

Baby
Bedtime Rhyme

461. Here is Bobby's Christmas tree

      FFr

Christmas
Christmas Tree
Counting

462. Here is brown bulb, small and round

      CCO

Flower
Plants and Seeds
Spring

463. Here is hungry Pig, Pig, Piggy Snout

      RFF, RRR

Animal Sounds
Cat, Cow, Pig, Sheep
Chicken
Counting

Index to Fingerplays

487. Here's a cup and here's a cup

    CCO, FiO, GFH,   Food
    LDF, RFF, RRR,   Kitchen Utensils or Dishes
    WDS   Manners
                            Sharing

488. Here's a donut big and fat

    ECT   Bread
                            Shape

489. Here's a great big hill with snow all over the side

    FPF, LDF, RRR,   Sports or Hobbies
    TCB   Winter

490. Here's a green leaf

    FFr, FPF, RFF,   Addition
    RRR   Flower
                            Plants and Seeds

491. Here's a little apple tree

    GFH, RRR   Apple Tree
                            Fall
                            Fruit
                            Size
                            Up and Down

492. Here's a little bunny on a shelf in the shop

    CCO   Store or Building
                            Toy

493. Here's a little wash bench

    LDF   Chores
                            Clothes

494. Here's a little washtub

    FFr, RFF, RRR   Chores
                            Clothes

Index to Fingerplays

504. Here's the baby's cradle where baby likes to sleep

      RFF

                            Animal Home
                            Baby
                            Bedtime Rhyme
                            Chicken
                            Counting
                            Sheep

505. Here's the doughnut

      RRR

                            Bread
                            Shape

506. He's got the whole world in His hands

      EWT (m)

                            Baby
                            Religious Rhyme

507. Hickory, dickory, dock! The mouse ran up the clock

      ADR, BFG, CCO,   Clock or Watch
      EWT (m), FFr, FFu,   Mother Goose Rhyme
      GDW (m), LDF, LiA,   Mouse
      MuF (m), PAT, PBS,   Telling Time
      Sta, TNT   Up and Down

508. High, high, high, up in the sky, the little birds fly

      FFr

                            Bedtime Rhyme
                            Bird
                            Left and Right, Up
                               and Down

509. Ho! Ho! Little folks do not be afraid

      FFr

                            Halloween
                            Jack-o-Lantern

510. Hold on tightly as we go

      LDF

                            High and Low
                            Playground
                            Safety Rule

Index to Fingerplays

519. Hush, little baby don't say a word

> ADR, EWT (m),
> GDW (m), TNT

> Baby
> Bedtime Rhyme
> Mother Goose Rhyme

I

520. I am a cobbler and this is what I do

> RRR

> Cobbler
> Shoes and Boots

521. I am a fine musician, I practice ev'ry day

> EWT (m)

> Musical Instrument

522. I am a fine musician, I travel round the world

> LDF

> Musical Instrument

523. I am a funny hoppity toad trying to jump across the road

> FiO

> Frog or Toad
> Insect

524. I am a little toad living by the road

> FFr, LiA, RFF

> Frog or Toad
> Insect
> Spring, Winter

525. I am a popcorn kernel

> ECT

> Left and Right
> Popcorn

526. I am a pumpkin, big and round

> FFr, HRh, RRR

> Halloween
> Jack-o-Lantern

Index to Fingerplays

536. I can make a hammock

    FFr

    Ball
Kitchen Utensils or Dishes
Structure

537. I can reach high, I can reach low

    FiO

    High and Low
Touching Rhyme

538. I can tie my shoelaces

    TNT

    Cleanliness
Dressing
Finger Rhyme
Shoes and Boots

539. I clap my hands

    RRR

    Touching Rhyme

540. I dig, dig, dig, and I plant some seeds

    RRR, TCB

    Plants and Seeds
Spring

541. I do the way my Daddy does when we go out to swim

    SAP

    Family
Sports or Hobbies

542. I dug in the sand

    MyB

    Counting
Sea and Seashore

543. I eat my peas with honey

    ADR, RRR

    Vegetable

544. I found a great big shell one day

    ECT, RRR

    Sea and Seashore
Senses

545. I go on a train that runs on a track

    ECT

    Train

Index to Fingerplays

546. I got to lick the batter bowl

    MUD

    Fast and Slow
    Food

547. I had a bird and the bird pleased me

    EWT (m)

    Animal Sounds
    Bird, Chicken, Duck, Goose
    Cow, Horse, Pig, Sheep

548. I had a little balloon that I hugged tight to me

    RRR

    Balloon

549. I had a little cherry stone

    GaY

    Fruit
    Plants and Seeds
    Tree

550. I had a little engine, but it wouldn't go

    GaY

    Airplane, Car, Train

551. I had a little husband

    TPM

    Mother Goose Rhyme
    Size

552. I had a little manikin

    TPM

    Size

553. I had a little monkey. He learned to climb a string

    LiA

    Health
    Manners
    Monkey
    Night Sky

554. I had a little monkey. His name was Slimsy Jim

    CCO

    Feelings
    Monkey

555. I had a little nut tree

      DEH (m)
                           Mother Goose Rhyme
                           Spain
                           Tree

556. I had a little poodle

      RRR
                           Dog

557. I had a little red balloon

      MyB
                           Balloon
                           Size

558. I had a little rooster and the rooster pleased me

      DEH (m)
                           Animal Sounds
                           Chicken, Duck
                           Dog
                           Tree

559. I have a dear little dolly

      RRR
                           Doll

560. I have a head and eyes that see

      WAI (m)
                           High and Low
                           Senses

561. I have a kitty cat named Puff

      RRR
                           Cat

562. I have a little cuckoo clock

      GaY
                           Clock or Watch
                           Counting
                           Telling Time

563. I have a little kitty

      FiO
                           Animal Sounds
                           Cat

564. I have a little toothbrush

      FiO
                           Health

74

573. I have ten little fingers, and they all belong to me

CCO, ECT, EWT (m),	Counting
FFr, FPF, GFH,	Hand Rhyme
LDF, MuF (m), PBS,	High and Low
RRR, WDS	Quiet Time Rhyme

574. I have ten little fingers, ten little toes

CCO, FFr	Counting
	Touching Rhyme

575. I have ten little fingers with which I like to play

LiA, PBS	Ant
	Counting
	Fish, Spider

576. I have two eyes to see with

RRR	Counting
	Senses
	Touching Rhyme

577. I have two friends and they have me

FiO	Counting
	Friendship

578. I hear thunder

GaY, GFH, Sta	Senses
	Thunderstorm

579. I heard a little tiny noise behind the cupboard door

GFH	Guessing Rhyme
	Mouse
	Senses

580. I help my family by sweeping the floor

ECT	Chores
	Helping Others

Index to Fingerplays

590. I like to peek inside a book

    RRR   Book

591. I like to pretend that I am a rose

    FFr, FiO, RFF,   Open and Shut
    RRR   Plants and Seeds
                                    Rose

592. I like to ride on a gallopy horse

    RRR   Horse

593. I listen to the raindrops fall

    RRR   Rain
                                    Senses

594. I looked in my looking glass

    ECT, RRR   Feelings
                                    Senses

595. I love my fingers, they're good and true

    SDG   Finger Rhyme
                                    High and Low

596. I love soft things so very much

    ECT, RRR   Feelings
                                    Senses
                                    Touching Rhyme

597. I love the mountains

    DEH (m)   Bird
                                    Daisy, Flower
                                    Field or Meadow, Mountain,
                                        Night Sky, Shadow
                                    Months and Days
                                    Summer
                                    Wind

598. I made a little snowman with hat and cane complete

    FFr   Snowman
                                    Winter

Index to Fingerplays

608. I saw a little ladybug flying in the air

    MiM

        Counting
        Insect

609. I saw a little rabbit come hop, hop, hop

    LiA

        Rabbit

610. I saw a rabbit; I said, "Hello"

    RRR

        Easter
        Rabbit (Easter)

611. I saw a slippery, slithery snake slide through the grasses, making them shake

    GaY

        Animal Sounds
        Snake

612. I say, "Hello," to my friends

    RRR, TCB

        Feelings
        Friendship

613. I see three—one, two, three

    FFr, RFF, RRR

        Bear, Cat, Frog or Toad, Rabbit
        Counting
        Duck

614. I shut the door and locked it tight

    LDF

        Door or Steps
        Open and Shut

615. I stretch my fingers away up high

    FFr, RFF

        Finger Rhyme
        Quiet Time Rhyme

616. I stuck my head in a little skunk's hole

    ECT, RRR

        Animal Home
        Guessing Rhyme
        Skunk

Index to Fingerplays

626. I wish I were a circus clown

    RRR

                       Clown
                       Feelings
                       Helping Others
                       Sharing
                       Wishing

627. I work in my garden

    FFr

                       Flower
                       Plants and Seeds
                       Rain, Sun
                       Spring

628. I'd like to surprise my mother, for this is Mother's Day

    SAP

                       Feelings
                       Mother's Day
                       Rose

629. If all the seas were one sea, what a great sea that would be

    CCO, LiB

                       Mother Goose Rhyme
                       Sea and Seashore
                       Size
                       Tool
                       Tree

630. If I could find old Santa, I'd ask him for a ride

    FFr

                       Christmas
                       Reindeer (Santa's)
                       Santa Claus

631. If I could have a windmill

    GaY

                       Animal Sounds
                       Duck, Goose
                       Store or Building
                       Water Bodies

632. If I had an airplane, zum, zum, zum, I'd fly to Mexico

    LDF, RRR

                       Airplane
                       Mexico

633. If I move one finger and wiggle my thumb, I'll have two fingers
     moving By Gum

       RRR   Counting
                                         Up and Down
                                       Quiet Time Rhyme

634. If I were a bird, I'd like to be a robin to fly

       SAP   Bird, Robin
                                       Wishing

635. If I were a bird, I'd sing a song

       ECT, RRR   Animal Home
                                       Bedtime Rhyme
                                       Bird
                                       Day and Night
                                       Quiet Time Rhyme

636. If I were a dentist, I know what I would do

       FPF   Doctor
                                       Health

637. If I were a farmer with flour, milk, and meat

       FiO   Farmer

638. If I were a horse—I'd neigh, of course

       LiB, FPF   Animal Sounds
                                       Bear, Horse, Pig, Snail,
                                           Chicken

639. If I were a little bird high up in the sky

       GaY   Bird
                                       Animal, Cat, Dog, Elephant,
                                           Giraffe, Kangaroo, Rabbit

640. If I were a little flower sleeping underneath the ground

       RRR, TCB   Flower
                                       Plants and Seeds
                                     Spring

641. If I were a witch, I'd ride on a broom

      LDF, FPF, TCB   Halloween
                                          Witch

642. If I were an apple and grew on a tree

      ECT, FFr   Apple Tree
                                          Fruit

643. If I'd put a feather in my hat, I'd look like Yankee Doodle

      LDF   Fourth of July
                                        Hat
                                        United States

644. If you spilled flour all over the floor

      ECT   Chores
                                        Helping Others
                                        Tool

645. If you were a beech tree, what would you

      GaY   Plants and Seeds
                                        Tree

646. If your fingers wiggle, cross them one by one

      RRR   Finger Rhyme

647. I'll be four-years-old next birthday

      RRR   Birthday
                                        Counting
                                        Hat

648. "I'll need—for April's thirty days," said little Isabella, "waterproof boots!"

      RRR   Clothes, Shoes and Boots
                                        Months and Days
                                        Spring

649. I'll pretend on Halloween that I'm a fancy king or queen

      CCO   Costume
                                        Halloween

Index to Fingerplays

650. I'll touch my hair, my lips, my eyes

      RRR   Touching Rhyme
                                                  Up and Down

651. I'm a bear—hear my growl

      RRR   Animal Sounds
                                                  Bear, Dog, Elephant, Lion,
                                                      Monkey
                                                  Senses

652. I'm a big, black engine on a long freight train

      SAP   Train
                                                  Up and Down

653. I'm a big spider

      CCO   Animal Home
                                                  Insect
                                                  Spider
                                                  Size

654. I'm a duck—I quack, quack, quack

      FPF   Animal Sounds
                                                  Day and Night
                                                  Duck
                                                  Water Bodies

655. I'm a friendly ghost—almost

      LDF   Ghost or Goblin
                                                  Halloween

656. I'm a little brown seed in the ground

      FFr, SAP   Plants and Seeds

657. I'm a little Christmas tree

      FPF   Christmas
                                                  Christmas Tree
                                                  Religious Rhyme

658. I'm a little doll who's been dropped and broken

      RRR

                              Christmas
                              Doll
                              Feelings

659. I'm a little hot dog

      MUD

                              Food

660. I'm a little robot short and square

      Sta

                              Machine
                              Size

661. I'm a little teapot, short and stout

      ADR, CCO, ECT,
      EWT (m), FFr,
      GaY, GFH, JTJ,
      LDF, MuF (m), PBS,
      PRh, ReG, RRR,
      SaG (m), Sta, TeF,
      TNT, WAA (m)

                              Kitchen Utensils or Dishes

662. I'm a puppet on a string

      MyB

                              Toy

663. I'm a scary ghost

      FPF

                              Feelings
                              Ghost or Goblin
                              Halloween

664. I'm all made of hinges and everything bends

      RRR

                              Concept
                              Structure

665. I'm an acorn, small and round

      EWT (m)

                              Squirrel
                              Plants and Seeds
                              Tree

666. I'm being swallowed by a boa constrictor

      GFH

                              Snake

677. I'm three years old

       LDF   Clothes
                                      Counting
                                      Dressing

678. In a green and yellow basket I found last Easter Day

       CCO   Easter
                                      Rabbit (Easter)

679. In a milkweed cradle snug and warm

       RRR   Plants and Seeds
                                      Wind

680. In and out, in and out, now I roll my hands about

       CCO   Hand Rhyme
                                      High and Low, In and Out

681. In faraway Australia, across the rolling sea, there lives the small koala
bear as cuddly as can be

       MyB   Animal
                                      Australia
                                      Tree

682. In Frisco Bay, there lived a whale

       DEH (m)   Animal
                                      Sea and Seashore
                                      United States

683. In my house are windows, two, shining clear and bright

       RRR   Open and Shut
                                      Store or Building

684. In my little garden bed raked so nicely over

       CCO, FFr, FiN (m),   Flower
       TeF   Plants and Seeds
                                      Rain, Sun
                                      Summer

Index to Fingerplays

J

710. Jack and Jill went up the hill

      CCO, ECT, EWT (m),   Mother Goose Rhyme
      FFr, GDW (m), LDF,   Up and Down
      TNT

711. Jack be nimble

      CCO, FFr, TNT   Mother Goose Rhyme

712. Jack Frost is a fairy small

      FFr   Jack Frost
                        Winter

713. Jack Frost paid me a visit

      FFr, RFF   Counting
                        Jack Frost
                        Months and Days
                        Shape
                        Winter

714. Jack-in-the-box all shut up tight, not a breath of air

      CCO, FFr, FPF,   Jack-in-the-Box
      LDF, RRR, TLB (m)

715. Jack-in-the-box all shut up tight. With the cover closed just right

      GFH, RRR   Jack-in-the Box

716. Jack-in-the-box Jack-in-the-Box. Wake up, wake up

      RRR   Counting
                        Jack-in-the-Box

717. Jack-in-the box sits so still

      ECT, TCB   Jack-in-the-Box
      GFH, RFF, RRR

718. Jack ran up to Jill's front door

      CCO   Friendship
                        Valentine's Day

Index to Fingerplays

719. Jelly on my head

    CCO   Food
                                  Touching Rhyme

720. Jenny Wren last week was wed

    RRR   Animal Home
                                  Counting
                                  Wren

721. Jesus loved children, one and all

    FPF   Religious Rhyme
                                  Size

722. Joan plays that she is Mommy

    RRR   Chores
                                  Family

723. John Brown had a little Indian

    CCO, GaY   Counting
                                  Indian

724. Johnny, Johnny

    FiR   Finger Rhyme
                                  Game

725. Johnny looked at the moon

    LiA, PBS   Astronaut
                                  Night Sky
                                  Rocket Ship

726. Johnny pounds with one hammer

    CCO, ECT, FPF,   Bedtime Rhyme
    LDF, MiM, RRR,   Counting
    TCB   Tool

727. Jump, jump, jump goes the big kangaroo

    FPF, RRR   Counting
                                  Kangaroo

K

728. A kitten is hiding under a chair

    FFr, GFH, LDF
                    Animal Sounds
                    Cat
                    Hiding

729. Kitty, kitty, kitty, kitty, all my little ones so pretty

    LDF
                    Animal Sounds
                    Cat

730. Knee-nicky-nack

    FuG
                    Touching Rhyme

731. Knock at the door

    GaY, LDF, PAT,
                    Tickling Rhyme
    SaG (m), TLB (m),
                    Touching Rhyme
    TNT

732. Knock, knock, knock *(Toc, toc, toc)

    *TLB (m)
                    *French Language Rhyme
                    Tickling Rhyme

733. Kookaburra sits in the old gum tree

    RRR
                    Australia
                    Counting Out

L

734. Laduski, ladushki! Where are you *(Laduski, ladushki! Gde byli)

    *TLB (m)
                    Baby, Grandparents
                    Food
                    Pat-a-Cake Rhyme
                    *Russian Language Rhyme

744. Let us chase the squirrel

    CCO   Squirrel
                                 Tree
                                 Up and Down

745. "Let us go to the wood," said this pig

    TPM   Counting
                                 Pig

746. Let us make a salad bowl

    MUD   Counting
                                 Vegetable

747. Let your hands go clap, clap, clap

    FFr, RRF, RRR   Counting
                                 Quiet Time Rhyme
                                 Up and Down

748. Let your hands so lightly clap, clap, clap.

    FFu, GaY, GFH,   Counting
    LDF, RRR   Hand Rhyme
                                 Quiet Time Rhyme

749. Let's all be a turkey fat

    MUD   Bread, Dessert, Food
                                 Thanksgiving
                                 Turkey

750. Let's build a house with bricks

    GFH   Counting
                                 Store or Building
                                 Wind

751. Let's drive our auto down the street

    LDF, RRR   Car
                                 Safety Rule

Index to Fingerplays

760. Lightning bolts shoot from the cloud

    FPF

Feelings
Thunderstorm

761. "A lion's knocking on my door"

    BPP

Animal Sounds
Lion

762. Listen, Mother, you know what

    RRR, TCB

Family
Feelings
Valentine's Day

763. Listen to the band parade

    ECT, RRR, TCB

Musical Instrument
Senses

764. Little airplane up in the sky, sometimes you're low, sometimes you're high

    FiO, FoD

Airplane
High and Low

765. Little Arabella Miller found a woolly caterpillar

    ADR, BPP,
    EWT (m), GaY,
    GFH

Butterfly and Caterpillar
Family

766. Little baby Moses in the rushes did float

    FPF

Baby
Religious Rhyme

767. A little ball, a bigger ball, a great big ball you see

    CCO, RFF

Ball
Counting
Size

768. Little Bear, Little Bear, turn around

    FFr

Bedtime Rhyme
Religious Rhyme
Teddy Bear

Index to Fingerplays

769. Little bears have three feet

      RRR, TCB   April Fools' Day
                                   Counting

770. Little Bo-Peep has lost her sheep

      DEH (m), FFr, FPF,   Mother Goose Rhyme
      RFF, TNT   Sheep

771. Little Boy Blue, come blow your horn

      CCO, FFr, LiB,   Cow, Sheep
      RFF, TNT   Mother Goose Rhyme
                                     Musical Instrument

772. Little boy-finger where have you been *(Pal'chik-mal'chik gde ty byl)

      *TLB (m)   Counting
                                     Finger Rhyme
                                   *Russian Language Rhyme

773. A little boy lived in this house

      LDF, PBS   Friendship
                                     Store or Building

774. A little boy went into a barn

      CCO   Mother Goose Rhyme
                                     Owl

775. The little boy (girl) went to look to find a turkey for the cook

      FPF   Animal Sounds
                                     Hiding
                                   Thanksgiving
                                   Turkey

776. A little boy (girl) went walking one lovely summer day

      CCO, ECT, FFu,   Animal Home
      FiN (m), FPF,   Earth and Sky, Water
      RRR, TCB   Bodies
                                   Fish, Rabbit
                                   Flower
                                   Insect
                                   Sparrow
                                   Store or Building
                                   Summer

777. A little brown bear went in search of some honey

      RRR   Bear
                                              Bee
                                              Senses

778. The little brown seed, so tiny and small, that was waiting under the ground

      SAP   Flower
                                                Plants and Seeds
                                              Rain, Sun

779. A little brown rabbit popped out of the ground

      GaY   Animal Home
                                                Rabbit

780. "Little brown sparrows flying around

      FiN (m)   Animal Home
                                                Sparrow
                                                Tree
                                                Up and Down

781. Little cabin in the woods

      BPP, PAT, RRR   Hunting
                                              Rabbit

782. The little candle burns so bright

      ECT   Bedtime Rhyme
                                                Safety Rule

783. Little canary yellowbreast sat upon a rail

      FPF   Bird

784. A little doggie all brown and black

      LDF   Dog

785. Little eyes see pretty things

      CCO   Senses
                                                Touching Rhyme

786. Little fish goes out to play

    LiA, RRR   Fish

787. Little friend just over the way

    RRR   Friendship

788. A little frog in a pond am I, hippity, hippity, hop. And I can jump in the air so high

    RRR   Frog or Toad

789. A little garden flower is lying in its bed

    RRR   Flower
                                            Plants and Seeds
                                            Rain, Sun
                                            Spring

790. A little green frog in a pond am I, hoppity, hoppity, hop. I sit on a little leaf high and dry

    GaY   Fish, Frog or Toad
                                              Water Bodies

791. The little grey squirrel searches around to find the nuts that have fallen down

    FPF   Fall, Winter
                                            Hiding
                                          Squirrel
                                            Tree

792. Little Jack Horner sat in a corner

    CCO, DEH (m), FFr,   Christmas
    LDF, RFF, TPM   Dessert, Fruit
                                              Mother Goose Rhyme

793. Little Jack Horner stood on the corner

    FFr   Left and Right
                                                Safety Rule

794. The little leaves are falling down

    LDF, RRR   Fall
                                              Tree

795. Little leaves fall gently down

      RFF, RRR, TCB   Color
                                          Fall
                                          Tree

796. Little Miss Muffet sat on a tuffet

      CCO, FFr, FPF,   Food
      PBS, RFF, TNT,   Mother Goose Rhyme
      TPM   Spider

797. A little monkey likes to do just the same as you and you

      FFr, RFF, RRR   Copy Cat Rhyme
                                          Game
                                          Monkey
                                          Up and Down

798. A little mouse came out to take a peek *(La petite souris a passe par ici)

      *RFF   Animal Sounds
                                          Counting
                                          *French Language Rhyme
                                          Mouse

799. A little mouse hid in a hole

      FPF   Cat, Mouse
                                          Hiding

800. "Little Nose." Where did you get that little red nose.

      FiO   Counting
                                          Jack Frost
                                          Senses

801. Little Peter Rabbit had a fly upon his nose

      DEH (m), SaG (m)   Insect
                                          Rabbit

802. Little piggy-wig on the farm close by

      GaY   Animal Sounds
                                          Bird
                                          Counting
                                          Cow, Dog, Pig, Sheep

803. Little Rabbit Foo Foo hopping through the forest

    DEH (m), RRR   Counting
                                   Fairy or Giant
                                   Rabbit, Mouse

804. Little red robins flying around

    MyB   Animal Home
                                   Robin
                                   Up and Down

805. Little Robin Redbreast sat upon a rail

    CCO, LDF, LiA,   Mother Goose Rhyme
    RFF   Robin

806. Little Robin Redbreast sat upon a tree

    CCO, FiP   Cat
                                   Mother Goose Rhyme
                                   Robin
                                   Up and Down

807. A little seed so soft and round

    FiO, FoD   Plants and Seeds
                                   Up and Down

808. The little snail is in no hurry

    FPF   Animal Home
                                   Manners
                                   Snail
                                   Store or Building

809. Little squirrel living there in the hollow tree

    FiN (m)   Animal Home
                                   Squirrel
                                   Tree

810. A little striped chipmunk sat up in a tree

    RFF   Animal
                                   Counting
                                   Tree

811. A little train stood on the track

     FFu, FPF   Train

812. The little white sheep went, "Baa"

     SAP   Animal Sounds
                                   Cat, Dog, Sheep

813. A little witch in a pointed cap on my door went rap, rap, rap

     CCO   Halloween
                                   Witch

814. Little white rabbit sits wiggling his ears *(Zaika belen'kii sidit)

     *TLB (m)   Feelings
                                   Rabbit
                                   *Russian Language Rhyme

815. London Bridge is falling down

     DEH (m), GaY,   Bridge
     GDW (m), PaR,   England
     ReG   Mother Goose Rhyme
                                   Up and Down

816. Look at my apple

     FoD   Division
                                   Fruit
                                   Shape
                                   Sharing

817. Look at the terrible crocodile

     GaY   Alligator or Crocodile, Fish
                                   Egypt
                                   Water Bodies

818. Look! I'm a dragon

     MyB   Airplane, Car
                                   Animal, Mouse
                                   Mountain, Night Sky
                                   Musical Instrument
                                   Store or Building

819. Love, love, love, love, the gospel in a word is love

      FPF   Religious Rhyme

M

820. Magalena Hagalena

      RRR   Color
                                          Counting
                                          Directions

821. Make a ball of soft, white snow

      RRR, TCB   Counting
                                          Size
                                          Snow, Sun
                                          Snowman
                                          Winter

822. Make a fist *(Musun-de)

      *TLB (m)   *Japanese Language Rhyme
                                          Touching Rhyme
                                          Up and Down

823. Make one eye go wink, wink, wink

      FFr, RFF, RRR   Counting
                                            Quiet Time Rhyme
                                          Senses

824. Many leaves are falling down

      LDF   Color
                                          Fall
                                          Tree

825. Master Thumb is first to come

      TPM   Counting
                                            Size

826. Matrioska Matrioska Matrioska dance dance

      BPP   Doll
                                          Russia

827. May Day, May Day, how do you do

      SmC   Flower
                                          Friendship
                                          May Day

828. May the road rise up to meet you

      BPP   Ireland
                                          Rain, Sun, Wind
                                          Religious Rhyme

829. The meenister in the poopit, he couldna say his prayers

      TPM   Career
                                          Religious Rhyme
                                          Scotland

830. A merry little river went singing day by day

      FiN (m)   Bread
                                          Store or Building
                                          Water Bodies

831. Merry little snowflakes falling through the air

      ECT, FFr, HRh,   Snow, Sun
      RFF, RRR   Spring, Winter

832. Michael, row the boat ashore, Hallelujah

      DEH (m)   Boat
                                          Water Bodies

833. Miss Lucy had a baby

      MuG (m)   Baby
                                          Pat-a-Cake Rhyme

834. Miss Mary Mack, Mack, Mack, all dressed in black, black, black

      DEH (m), MuG (m)   Pat-a-Cake Rhyme

844. Mix the batter

    RRR   Dessert

845. Mommy put some corn flakes in my favorite bowl

    MUD   Food

846. Monday's child is fair of face

    CCO, TNT   Months and Days
                                Mother Goose Rhyme

847. Monkey, monkey in the tree, I see you and you see me

    FP1   Monkey

848. The month is October

    LDF   Color
                                Fall
                                Months and Days
                                Tree

849. Morning comes on quiet feet

    MyB   Nature

850. Mother, Father, Sister, Brother Baby, too, will pray

    FFr, RFF, TCB   Family
                                Religious Rhyme
                                Thanksgiving

851. Mother Hen walks proudly

    SAP   Animal Sounds
                                Chicken
                                Counting

852. Mother plays the violin

    ECT, RRR   Family
                                Musical Instrument

853. Mother's washing

    GaY   Chores
                                Clothes
                                Family

854. A mountain beautiful am I

    BPP   Mountain

855. A mouse lived in a little hole

    FPF, GaY   Animal Home
                                         Mouse

856. Move like this this this Little puppets, little puppets *(Ainsi font font font Les petites marionnettes)

    TLB (m)   *French Language Rhyme
                                         Toy

857. Mrs. Peck Pigeon is pecking for bread

    FFr   Counting
                                         Pigeon
                                         Up and Down

858. Mrs. Pussy, nice and fat, with her kittens four

    FiN (m), RRR, TeF   Addition, Counting
                                         Cat, Mouse

859. The mule has two long ears

    FuG   Animal Sounds
                                         Horse

860. Mummy has scissors, snip, snip, snip

    GaY   Clothes
                                         Counting
                                         Craft
                                         Family

861. My birthday cake is pink and white

    FFr, RFF   Birthday
                                         Counting
                                         Dessert

862. "My bunnies now must go to bed," the little mother rabbit said

    LDF   Bedtime Rhyme
                                         Counting
                                         Rabbit

863. My Christmas tree is nice and bright

      FiO

                             Christmas
                             Christmas Tree
                             Santa Claus

864. My Daddy's saw sings a funny song

      FuG

                             Family
                             Tool

865. My darling little goldfish hasn't any toes

      CCO

                             Fish

866. My dog, Duke, knows many tricks

      SAP

                             Dog
                             Friendship
                             Game

867. My dolly is a lady

      RRR

                             Doll
                             Feelings
                             Manners

868. My eyes can see

      JTJ, RRR

                             Senses

869. My father bought a pumpkin

      ECT

                             Dessert
                             Halloween, Thanksgiving

870. My father said, "It's doctor day"

      ECT

                             Doctor
                             Health
                             Helping Others

871. My fingers are so sleepy

      FiR, LDF

                             Bedtime Rhyme
                             Counting
                             Finger Rhyme

880. My little jalopy is a right good friend

      RRR   Car
                                            Counting
                                            Money

881. My little rabbit does not have much fun *(Mon petit lapin a bien du chagrin)

      RFF   *French Language Rhyme
                                            Rabbit

882. My mama told ME

      FP2   Copy Cat Rhyme
                                            Up and Down

883. My mother knits my mittens

      FuG   Craft
                                            Clothes, Mittens
                                            Family

884. My mother (father) said, "It's doctor day"

      ECT, RRR   Doctor
                                          Health

885. My nose can't smell

      FPF   Health
                                            Manners
                                            Senses
                                            Touching Rhyme

886. My pigeon house I open wide

      FFr, GaY   Animal Sounds
                                            Bedtime Rhyme
                                          Finger Rhyme
                                          Pigeon

887. My rabbit has two big ears

      LDF   Rabbit

N

896. Nose, nose, nose, mouth *(Hana, hana, hana, kucki)

      *RRF   *Japanese Language Rhyme
                                             Senses
                                             Touching Rhyme

897. Now I am a snowman

      FFr   Snowman
                                             Winter

898. Now I lay me down to sleep

      FPF   Bedtime Rhyme
                                             Religious Rhyme

899. Now I will play my little horn

      RRR   Musical Instrument

900. Now I'll tell you a story and this story is new

      GaY   Counting
                                             Following Commands
                                             Mouse
                                             Store or Building

901. Now let us clasp our little hands

      RRR   Bedtime Rhyme
                                             Religious Rhyme

902. Now my hands are on my head

      CCO   Quiet Time Rhyme
                                             Touching Rhyme

903. Now put away your sled

      TCB   Spring

O

912. Oh, we skip round the pot

> MUD

Kitchen Utensils or Dishes
Size

913. Oh, what shall we do in our garden this fine day

> GaY

Plants and Seeds
Tool

914. Oh, when you clap, clap, clap your hands

> RRR

Copy Cat Rhyme

915. Oh! Where are the merry, merry Little Men to join us in our play

> FiN (m)

Finger Rhyme
Size

916. Oh! Where do you come from, you little drops of rain

> FFr

Rain

917. Oh, you funny, funny snowman

> GFH

Size
Snowman
Winter

918. Ohhh—a churning we will go

> RRR

Food

919. Old Bumblebee came out of the barn

> BPP

Animal Sounds
Bee
Tickling Rhyme

920. Old Dan has two eyes

> RRR

Horse
Touching Rhyme

921. Old Davy Jones had one little sailor

> TPM

Countdown, Counting
Sailor

Index to Fingerplays

922. Old Jack Frost came last night

     FPF   Jack Frost
                                                  Winter

923. Old John Muddlecombe lost his cap

     GaY, Sta   Hat
                                                  Remembering

924. Old MacDonald had a farm, E-I-E-I-O

     EWT (m), GaY,   Animal Sounds
     GDW (m), TNT   Chicken, Duck
                                                  Cow, Horse, Pig

925. Old man Chang, I've often heard it said *(Lao Zhang, Lao Zhang)

     *TLB (m)   China
                                                  *Chinese Language Rhyme
                                                  Tickling Rhyme

926. Old Mr. Pumpkin hiding in a box

     CCO   Fall
                                                   Fruit
                                                  Halloween

927. Old Mister Rabbit had a mighty habit

     FiP   Hand Rhyme
                                                  Rabbit
                                                  Vegetable

928. Old Ned had two ears that go flop, flop, flop

     CCO   Counting
                                                   Horse

929. The old scarecrow is such a funny man

     FPF   Back and Forth, Left
                                                     and Right
                                                  Crow
                                                  Scarecrow

930. Old shoes, new shoes

      LDF

          Color
          Counting
          Shoes and Boots

931. Old Tom Tomato like a red ball

      GaY

          Fruit
          Shape

932. On Easter day, we go to church

      FFr, RFF

          Bell
          Easter
          Religious Rhyme
          Store or Building

933. On Easter morning the sun comes up

      MiM

          Color
          Counting
          Easter
          Eggs
          Rabbit (Easter)
          Sun

934. On Halloween, just take a peek

      FFr

          Fairy or Giant
          Halloween
          Witch

935. On Halloween night, five little ghosts went out to have a
    marshmallow roast

      MUD

          Counting
          Food
          Ghost or Goblin
          Halloween

936. On my face I have a nose

      FiO

          Counting
          Senses
          Touching Rhyme

Index to Fingerplays

937. On my Jack-o-lantern I will put great eyes

      CCO   Halloween
                                                 Jack-o-Lantern

938. On sunny days I go to play

      ECT   Sports or Hobbies

939. On the roof just over head patter goes the rain

      SAP   Clothes, Shoes and Boots
                                                 Rain

940. On top of spaghetti all covered with cheese

      EWT (m), TOB (m)   Food

941. Once I saw a beehive out in the maple tree

      RFF   Animal Home
                                                 Animal Sounds
                                                 Counting
                                                 Bee
                                                 Tree

942. Once I saw a bunny and a green, green cabbage head

      LDF, RRR   Rabbit
                                                 Vegetable

943. Once I saw a little bird

      RRR, TPM   Bird

944. Once I saw an ant hill

      CCO, FiN (m), RRR,   Animal Home
      TeF   Ant
                                                 Counting

945. Once there was a bunny

      FFr, RFF   Rabbit
                                                 Vegetable

946. Once there was a pumpkin

       FFr

                                             Fruit
                                             Halloween
                                             Jack-o-Lantern
                                             Plants and Seeds

947. Once there was a snowman

       CCO, FFr

                                             Snowman
                                             Wind
                                             Winter

948. Once there were ten little children

       RRR

                                             Chores
                                             Counting
                                             Family
                                             Feelings
                                             Helping Others

949. One and one are two. That I always knew

       RFF   Addition

950. One baby turtle alone and new

       MiM

                                             Counting
                                             Turtle

951. One bottle pop, two bottle pop

       DEH (m)

                                             Food
                                             Counting

952. One day as I was riding on the subway

       DEH (m)

                                             Hat
                                             Size
                                             Vehicle

953. One day I got up early

       SAP

                                             Chores
                                             Cleanliness
                                             Family
                                             Helping Others

Index to Fingerplays

962. One friendly dinosaur wanted to play peek-a-boo

      FPF

      Counting
      Dinosaur
      Hiding
      Peek-a-Boo Rhyme

963. One, I see

      LDF

      Counting
      United States

964. One is a cat that says meow

      MyB

      Animal Sounds
      Cat, Cow, Dog, Sheep
      Chicken, Crow
      Counting

965. One is for your heart so true

      CCO

      Counting
      Valentine's Day

966. One is the engine, shiny and fine

      FFr, RFF

      Counting
      Train

967. One kitten with a furry tail

      RFF

      Cat
      Counting

968. One light, two light, three lights, and four

      RFF

      Addition, Counting
      Candle
      Finger Rhyme
      Hanukkah

969. One little baby rocking in a tree

      HRh, LiB, MiM,
      RRR

      Baby
      Counting
      Peek-a-Boo Rhyme

Index to Fingerplays

978. One little turtle feeling so blue

FiO, RFF — Counting, Turtle

979. One little, two little, three little hunters

RRR — Countdown, Counting, Hunting

980. One little, two little, three little Indians

EWT (m), FFr, LDF — Countdown, Counting, Indian

981. One little, two little, three little kittens

RRR — Cat, Dog, Counting

982. One little, two little, three little monkeys

RRR — Counting, Friendship, Monkey

983. One little, two little, three little snowmen

FFr, RFF — Countdown, Counting, Snowman, Winter

984. One little, two little, three little witches

FFr, FPF, LDF, RFF, TCB — Counting, Halloween, Night Sky, Witch

985. One little valentine said, "I love you"

RFF — Counting, Feelings, Valentine's Day

Index to Fingerplays

1011. One, two, three, four, five in a row

      FFr, RFF   Counting
                                   Soldier

1012. One, two, three, four, five little reindeer stand by the gate

      FFr, FiO, RFF   Addition, Counting
                                   Christmas
                                   Reindeer (Santa's)
                                   Santa Claus

1013. One, two, three, four, five. Five little squirrels sitting in a tree

      LDF   Counting
                                   Hunting
                                   Squirrel

1014. One, two, three, four, five, six, seven, all good children go to Devon

      LDF   Counting Out
                                   England
                                   Spelling Rhyme

1015. One, two, three, four, five, six, seven, eight, nine. See the dresses on the clothesline

      RFF   Clothes
                                   Counting

1016. One, two, three, four, five, when will the valentines arrive

      CCO   Counting
                                   Mail
                                   Valentine's Day

1017. 1, 2, 3, 4, Mary at the kitchen door

      LDF, TNT   Counting
                                   Fruit

1018. One, two, three, four, these little pussy cats came to my door

      FFr, GaY   Cat
                                   Counting

Index to Fingerplays

1019. One, two, three little chickens

      LDF

           Animal Sounds
           Bedtime Rhyme
           Chicken
           Counting

1020. 1, 2, 3, there's a bug on me

      RRR

           Counting
           Insect

1021. One, two, three, to the woods goes she *(Un, deux, trois, j'irai dans le bois)

      *RFF

           Counting
           *French Language Rhyme
           Fruit

1022. One, two, what shall we do

      FP2

           Counting
           Quiet Time Rhyme

1023. One wheel, two wheels on the ground

      PRh, RFF, RRR

           Counting
           Bicycle

1024. One-ry, two-ry, dickery seven

      StD (m)

           Counting Out
           Pat-a-Cake Rhyme

1025. Open, shut them, open, shut them, give them a little clap

      CCO, FFr, FiO,
      FPF, LDF, MyB,
      PAT, RFF, RRR,
      SDG (m)

           Fast and Slow, Open
             and Shut,
           Up and Down
           Following Commands
           Hand Rhyme

1026. Open the car door, climb inside

      RRR

           Car
           Safety Rule

1027. The organ man, the organ man, is standing in the street

    CCO
                         Career
                         Monkey
                         Musical Instrument

1028. Our turkey is a big fat bird

    CCO — Thanksgiving, Turkey

1029. Out in the garden where the cabbages grow

    RRR — Animal Sounds, Dog, Rabbit, Vegetable

1030. Outside the door the bare tree stands

    FFr — Tree, Winter

1031. Over in the meadow, in the sand, in the sun, lived an old mother toad and her toadie one

    DEH (m), LiA — Day and Night, Field or Meadow, Night Sky, Frog or Toad, Sun

1032. Over the hills and far away

    LiB — Senses

1033. Over there the sun gets up

    ECT, RRR — Day and Night, Sun

1034. An owl sat alone on the branch of a tree

    CCO, LiA, FFr, RFF, RRR — Animal Sounds, Fairy or Giant, Halloween, Night Sky, Owl, Quiet Time Rhyme, Tree

1035. The owl's eyes open wide at night

   BPP

   Animal Sounds
   Left and Right
   Owl

P

1036. *Pao Pao Pao (No English Version)

   *TLB

   Ant
   *Dioula Language Rhyme
   Ivory Coast
   Pat-a-Cake Rhyme
   Tickling Rhyme

1037. Pat-a-cake, pat-a-cake, baker's man

   ADR, CCO, EWT (m),
   FFr, FuG, FPF,
   GaY, LDF, MuF (m),
   PAT, RFF, StD (m),
   TeF, TLB (m), TNT,
   TTB

   Dessert
   Mother Goose Rhyme
   Pat-a-Cake Rhyme

1038. Pat a cake, pat a cake, little girl fair *(Guang-guang cha)

   *TLB (m)

   China
   *Chinese Language Rhyme
   Pat-a-Cake Rhyme

1039. Patrick is a leprechaun

   TCB

   Fairy or Giant
   St. Patrick's Day

1040. Peace is my dream

   FPF

   Peace

1041. Pease porridge hot

  ADR, CCO, FuG,   Food
  LDF, MUD, PAT,   Opposites
  TLB (m), TNT,   Pat-a-Cake Rhyme
  WAA (m)

1042. Peekaboo, I see you

  FPF   Peek-a-Boo Rhyme

1043. Peek-a-boo, peek-a-boo

  GaY, TLB (m)   Hiding
                                Peek-a-Boo Rhyme

1044. "Peep, peep, peep," says the little chicken yellow

  FFu   Animal Sounds
                                Chicken

1045. Peter hammers with one hammer

  EWT (m), GaY,   Counting
  Sta   Tool

1046. Pick an orange

  MUD   Food, Fruit
                                Division

1047. Pick up some snow; pack it hard and round

  SAP   Counting
                                Family
                                Size
                                Snow
                                Snowman
                                Winter

1048. Piggie Wig and Piggie Wee

  CCO, FiN (m), FFr   Manners
                                Pig

1058. Policeman stands so tall and straight

    ECT, RRR

                        Car
                        Career, Mail Carrier, Police
                            Officer
                        Friendship
                        Helping Others
                        Mail
                        Safety Rule

1059. Polly had a birthday

    FFr, RFF, RRR

                        Birthday
                        Candle
                        Counting
                        Dessert
                        Guessing Rhyme

1060. Polly put the kettle on

    DEH (m), TPM

                        Food
                        Kitchen Utensils or Dishes
                        Mother Goose Rhyme

1061. Poor old Jonathan Bing

    LDF

                        Clothes, Hat
                        Remembering

1062. Popcorn, popping, pop, pop, pop

    FPF

                        Popcorn

1063. Pop! Pop! Pop! Pour the corn into the pot

    FFr

                        Popcorn

1064. Pot on the stove goes bubble, bubble, s-s-s-s

    MUD

                        Food
                        Kitchen Utensils or Dishes
                        Senses

1065. Pound pound pound pound goes the hammer

    LDF

                        Tool

Index to Fingerplays

1076. Put your finger on your nose

    BPP

                                  Finger Rhyme
                                  Senses
                                  Touching Rhyme

R

1077. Rabbit ain't got no tail at all

    DEH (m), RRR   Rabbit

1078. A rabbit came to my house once with funny, stretched-out ears

    FFr

                                    Easter
                                    Feelings
                                    Rabbit (Easter)

1079. Rabbit in a hollow sits and sleeps

    GaY

                                    Animal Home
                                    Hunting
                                    Rabbit

1080. The raccoon tail am ringy round

    FP1

                                    Animal, Rabbit
                                    United States

1081. The rain is dripping from the eaves

    SAP

                                    Clothes, Hat, Shoes and
                                      Boots
                                    Rain
                                    Touching Rhyme

1082. Rain is falling down

    LDF   Rain

1083. Rain on green grass

    RRR, Sta, TCB   Rain

1092. Ride with me on the merry-go-round

      ECT, FFr, RFF,   Circus or Carnival
      RRR   Up and Down

1093. Right foot, left foot, see me go

      ECT, PRh, RRR   Elephant
                             Guessing Rhyme
                             Left and Right
                             Size

1094. Right hand, left hand, put them on my head

      CCO   Bedtime Rhyme
                             Left and Right
                             Touching Rhyme

1095. Ring, ring, ring the bells

      FPF, RRR   Bell
                             Christmas

1096. Ring the bell, knock at the door

      TTB   Tickling Rhyme
                             Touching Rhyme

1097. Ring the bells for Merry Christmas

      SAP   Bell
                             Christmas
                             Christmas Tree

1098. Robbie the Rabbit is fat, fat, fat

      FFr   Rabbit

1099. Robin, Robin, Redbreast sits on a rail

      TPM   Robin

1100. Robot, robot, do as I command

      FPF   Copy Cat Rhyme
                             Machine
                             Quiet Time Rhyme

Index to Fingerplays

1101. Rockabye baby in the tree top *(Moe moe pepe tumutumu o laua)

CCO, GDW (m), LDF, SDG (m), *TLB (m)	Baby Mother Goose Rhyme *Samoan Language Rhyme Tree Wind

1102. Rock-a-bye baby, thy cradle is green

LDF, TLB (m)	Baby Mother Goose Rhyme

1103. Roll a roll

MUD	Copy Cat Rhyme Dessert

1104. Roll a snowball large

FFr, FiO, RFF, RRR	Shape Size Snowman Touching Rhyme Winter

1105. Roll a snowball round and round

CCO	Counting Snow, Sun Snowman Winter

1106. Roll him and roll him until he is big

HRh, RRR	Size Snowman Winter

1107. Roll, roll, roll your hands

CCO, FiO, FPF, RFF, RRR	Fast and Slow Following Commands Hand Rhyme

1108. Roll the snow over and over

    RRR   Counting
                                                 Snow
                                                 Snowman
                                                 Winter

1109. Roly-poly caterpillar into a room crept

    FFr, GFH   Animal Home
                                               Butterfly and Caterpillar

1110. Roly poly, ever so slowly

    GaY   Fast and Slow
                                              Hand Rhyme

1111. Roly poly, roly poly, up, up, up

    GaY   Hand Rhyme
                                             In and Out, Up and Down

1112. Round about, round about, catch a wee mouse

    TTB   Mouse
                                             Touching Rhyme

1113. Round about the rosebush

    TTB   Counting
                                             Rose
                                             Touching Rhyme

1114. Round about there sat a little hare

    TTB   Animal, Dog
                                             Touching Rhyme

1115. Round and round the garden

    ADR, GaY, TLB (m),   Teddy Bear
    TNT, TTB   Tickling Rhyme

1116. Round and round the haystack

    GaY, TLB (m)   Mouse
                                            Tickling Rhyme

1117. Row, row a-fishing we'll go

    CCO

                                  Counting
                                  Family
                                  Food
                                  Sports or Hobbies

1118. Row, row, row your boat

    ADR, GaY, LiB,   Boat
    LDF, RRR, TNT   Water Bodies

1119. Rub-a-dub dub, three men in a tub

    ADR, TNT   Counting

1120. Run, little rabbit *(Conejito que corre)

    *RFF   Chile
                                    Rabbit
                                  *Spanish Language Rhyme

S

1121. Said the farmer, the miller, the baker, "We'll give the dear baby his food"

    CCO   Car
                                    Carpenter, Cobbler, Farmer
                                  Counting

1122. Said the first little chicken

    CCO, LiA   Chicken
                                    Counting

1123. Said the first little snowflake

    FFr   Counting
                                    Snow
                                  Winter

1124. Said the kind kangaroo, "What can I do"

    FFr   Counting
                                    Kangaroo

1125. Said this little fairy, "I'm as thirsty as can be"

    LDF

                              Counting
                              Fairy or Giant

1126. Said this little fairy, "I'm as tired as can be"

    RFF, RRR

                              Bedtime Rhyme
                              Counting
                              Fairy or Giant

1127. Sailing in the boat when the tide runs high

    EWT (m)

                              Boat
                              Friendship
                              Sea and Seashore

1128. A sailor went to sea, sea, sea

    MuG (m)

                              Pat-a-Cake Rhyme
                              Sailor
                              Sea and Seashore

1129. Salutation to Ganesha *(Namo Ganesha)

    *TLB (m)

                              *Hindi Language Rhyme
                              India
                              Religious Rhyme

1130. Salute to the Captain

    CCO

                              Opposites

1131. Santa Claus will soon be here

    CCO

                              Christmas
                              Counting
                              Family
                              Santa Claus

1132. Scarecrow, scarecrow, turn around

    TCB

                              Halloween
                              Scarecrow

1133. The seals all flap their shining flips

    FFr

                              Animal

1142. See the little rabbit with his big long ears

    FFu, RRR   Rabbit
                                                Senses

1143. See the window I have here

    LDF, RRR   Senses
                                                Shape
                                              Store or Building

1144. See them dance, so! so!

    RRR   Toy

1145. See this finger! It is Sue

    RRR   Friendship

1146. See-saw, see-saw, up and down we go

    RFF   High and Low, Up
                                                    and Down
                                                Playground

1147. See-saw! The woodmen work. The woodmen of San Juan *(Aserrin! Aserran! Los maderos de San Juan)

    *RFF   Career
                                                Colombia
                                              Counting
                                              *Spanish Language Rhyme

1148. Seven little candles all in a line

    SmC   Candle
                                                  Counting
                                                Kwanzaa

1149. Shake, shake, knock, knock

    LDF   Musical Instrument

1150. Shake the walnut tree

    SAP   Tree

Index to Fingerplays

1151. Shake them, shake them, give a little clap

        CCO

                                  Clothes
                                  Hand Rhyme
                                  Peek-a-Boo Rhyme

1152. She runs for Daddy's slippers

        RRR

                                  Family
                                  Feelings
                                  Helping Others
                                  Manners

1153. She sailed away on a lovely summer's day

        DEH (m), PRh,
        RRR

                                  Alligator or Crocodile
                                  Egypt
                                  Water Bodies

1154. She'll be coming round the mountain when she comes, Toot, Toot

        BFG, GDW (m),
        GaY, PaR

                                  Chicken
                                  Food
                                  Horse
                                  Mountain

1155. Shhhh . . .be very quiet

        RRR

                                  Quiet Time Rhyme

1156. Show me one hand

        FFr

                                  Counting
                                  Following Commands
                                  Touching Rhyme

1157. A shy little ground hog left his bed

        TCB

                                  Animal
                                  Animal Home
                                  Ground-hog Day
                                  Left and Right
                                  Shadow
                                  Sun

1158. Sift the flour and break an egg

        RRR, TCB

                                  Birthday
                                  Dessert

1159. Silly little Teddy Bear stood up in a rocking chair

    FFr

Safety Rule
Teddy Bear

1160. Simon took his hook and pole

    RRR

Food
Health
Sports or Hobbies

1161. Sing a song of popcorn

    FFr

Counting
Popcorn

1162. Sing a song of sixpence a pocket full of rye

    CCO, FFr, LDF,
    PAT, RFF, TNT

Blackbird
Bread, Dessert
Money
Mother Goose Rhyme
Opposites

1163. Six little candles on a birthday cake

    RFF

Birthday
Candle
Countdown
Dessert

1164. Six little ducks that I once knew

    SaG (m)

Animal Sounds
Counting
Duck
Size

1165. Six little ducks without a shoe

    CCO

Counting
Duck
Size

1166. Six little snails lived in a tree

    GaY

Counting, Subtraction
Snail

Index to Fingerplays

1167. Skim, skim, skim, with the skimmer bright
FiN (m)   Food

1168. A sledding we will go
SmC   Animal, Bear, Dog, Fish
                                     Animal Sounds
                                     Snow
                                     Sports or Hobbies

1169. Slice, slice, the bread looks nice
GaY   Bread

1170. Slide your fingers into the wide part
LDF   Mittens
                                     Winter

1171. Slip on your raincoat
ECT, RRR, TCB   Clothes, Shoes and Boots
                                     Rain

1172. Slowly, slowly, very slowly creeps the garden snail
GaY, TLB (m)   Fast and Slow
                                     Mouse, Snail
                                     Tickling Rhyme

1173. Smile when you're happy
ECT   Feelings

1174. The snail is so slow
LDF, TLB (m)   Snail
                                     Tickling Rhyme

1175. Snip, snip, snip, snippety
LDF   Health

1176. Snip, snip, snip the paper
LDF   Craft
                                     Valentine's Day

1177. Snow piled up will make a hill

      FFr

                                    Size
                                    Snow
                                    Sports or Hobbies
                                    Winter

1178. Snowflakes dancing merrily

      SAP

                                    Snow
                                    Winter

1179. Snowflakes whirling all around

      FPF, LDF, PBS

                                    Snow
                                    Winter

1180. So many children/ it's going to be fun

      ECT

                                    Friendship

1181. Soft kitty, warm kitty

      ECT, RRR

                                    Cat

1182. Softly—softly, at the close of day, little mice come creeping from their homes to play

      RRR

                                    Cat, Mouse

1183. Softly, softly creeps the pussy cat

      FFr

                                    Cat, Rabbit
                                    Quiet Time Rhyme

1184. Softly, softly falling so, this is how the snowflakes go

      GaY

                                    Rain, Snow
                                    Spring, Winter

1185. Some boats are big

      ECT

                                    Boat
                                    Size

1186. Some folks wash with a washer

      SAP

                                    Chores
                                    Machine

1196. Start with a very tiny ball, roll it through the snow

      FFr   Size
                                     Snow
                                     Snowman
                                     Winter

1197. The steam shovel scoop opens its mouth so wide

      ECT, GFH, LDF,   Machine
      RRR   Vehicle

1198. Stir the pot of porridge

      FuG   Food

1199. Stop on the corner watch for the light

      ECT, FFr   Left and Right
                                     Safety Rule

1200. "Stop" says the red light

      CCO   Safety Rule

1201. The storm came up so very quick

      FFr   Rain

1202. Such jolly fun to rake the leaves

      FFr   Chores
                                     Fall
                                     Safety Rule

1203. The sweet chocolate bunny poked out his head

      FFr   Easter
                                     Food

1204. Swim, little fish, in water clear

      GaY   Bedtime Rhyme
                                     Bird
                                     Butterfly and Caterpillar
                                     Fish

T

1213. Teddybear, teddybear, dance on your toes

      TNT

      Bedtime Rhyme
      Teddy Bear
      Touching Rhyme

1214. Teddy bear, teddy bear, turn around

      BPP, CCO, ECT,
      FP1, GFH, PBS,
      PRh, RRR, TOB (m)

      Bedtime Rhyme
      Teddy Bear

1215. Teddy Bear went climbing

      SAP

      Teddy Bear

1216. Ten circus wagons painted oh so gay

      FFr, RFF

      Animal, Elephant, Lion,
        Monkey
      Circus or Carnival
      Counting

1217. Ten fat sausages sizzling in the pan

      ADR, GaY
      Food

      Countdown

1218. Ten fat turkeys standing in a row

      CCO

      Counting
      Hunting
      Left and Right
      Thanksgiving
      Turkey

1219. Ten fingers are a lot of fun

      RRR

      Clothes
      Counting
      Feelings
      Health
      Manners
      Religious Rhyme

Index to Fingerplays

1236. Ten little finger soldiers standing in a row

       RRR, TCB   Counting
                                          High and Low, Up
                                            and Down

1237. Ten little firemen sleeping in a row

       CCO, GFH, FFr,   Counting
       FPF, LDF, RRR   Fire Engine
                                                Fire Fighter

1238. Ten little fishes swim to and fro

       CCO   Bird
                                            Counting
                                          Fish, Mouse

1239. Ten little fishes were swimming in a school

       LDF, WDS   Counting
                                          Fish

1240. Ten little froggies were swimming in a pool

       FFr, RFF   Counting
                                          Frog or Toad

1241. Ten little gentlemen standing in a row

       GaY   Counting
                                            Manners

1242. Ten little goblins dancing in a ring

       RRR   Counting
                                            Ghost or Goblin
                                            Halloween
                                          Quiet Time Rhyme
                                          Senses

1243. Ten little grasshoppers sitting on a vine

       LDF, RFF   Countdown
                                          Insect

1277. There was a bunny who lived in the wood

    FFr   Rabbit

1278. There was a farmer had a dog, and Bingo was his name O

    EWT (m), GDW (m),   Dog
    MuF (m), RRR,   Spelling Rhyme
    TOB (m)

1279. There was a field that waiting lay

    FiN (m)   Crow
                                      Fall, Spring
                                      Farmer
                                      Field or Meadow, Plants
                                          and Seeds
                                      Hunting
                                      Rain, Sun

1280. There was a funny little man in a funny little house

    CCO, FFr, RFF,   Finger Rhyme
    RRR   High and Low, In and Out,
                                          Up and Down
                                      Store or Building

1281. There was a great big stilt man who was tall, t-a-l-l, t-a-l-l

    LDF   Circus or Carnival
                                        Size

1282. There was a little bunny who lived in the wood

    HRh, RRR   Rabbit

1283. There was a grasshopper that was always on the jump

    ADR   Insect

1284. There was a little hole and a mouse crept in

    RRR   Cat, Mouse

1285. There was a little turtle who lived in a box

    EWT (m), FFr, FiR,   Animal Home
    FPF, GFH, JTJ,   Turtle
    LDF, RRR

1294. There's a hole in the bottom of the sea

    EWT (m)   Sea and Seashore

1295. There's a little white duck sitting in the water

    EWT (m)   Animal Sounds
                                        Duck
                                        Feelings
                                        Flower
                                        Frog or Toad, Snake
                                        Insect
                                        Water Bodies

1296. There's such a tiny little mouse

    GaY, PBS   Day and Night
                                          Mouse

1297. These are the brown leaves fluttering down

    RRR, TCB   Animal Home
                                          Fall, Winter
                                            Squirrel
                                            Tree

1298. These five little playmates live here

    RRR   Counting
                                            Friendship
                                          High and Low, Up
                                                and Down

1299. They call me Little Sleepy Head

    FFr   Quiet Time Rhyme

1300. They do so, so, so

    LDF   Counting
                                            Finger Rhyme

1301. They say that daisies will not tell

    RRR   Daisy

1310. This is a forest of long long ago

      CCO

Counting
Hiding
Indian
Tree

1311. This is a nest for Mr. Bluebird

      RRR

Animal Home
Bee
Bird
Rabbit

1312. This is a pussy, sleek and gray

      FFr

Bedtime Rhyme
Cat
Counting
Quiet Time Rhyme

1313. This is a very nice jack-o-lantern

      LDF

Halloween
Jack-o-Lantern

1314. This is Brownie's dog house

      CCO, RFF

Animal Home
Dog
Helping Others

1315. This is East and this is West

      FFr

Bedtime Rhyme
Directions
High and Low, Narrow
  and Wide,
Open and Shut, Up
  and Down
Touching Rhyme

1316. This is grandpa's smoking pipe

      FuG

Grandparents
Health

Index to Fingerplays

1317. This is high and this is low

    CCO

    Counting
    Hand Rhyme
    High and Low, Left and
        Right,
    Narrow and Wide, Up
        and Down

1318. This is how the snowflakes play about

    GaY

    In and Out
    Snow, Sun
    Winter

1319. This is how we blow our balloons

    ECT, LDF, RRR

    Balloon

1320. This is Jack in a box

    LiA

    Jack-in-the-Box

1321. This is little mousie running round and round

    FuG

    Mouse
    Tickling Rhyme

1322. This is little Timothy Snail

    GaY

    Animal Home
    Feelings
    Snail

1323. This is little Tommy Thumb

    CCO, LDF, RRR

    Counting
    Size

1324. This is mother

    CCO, FP2, LDF

    Counting
    Family
    Size

1325. This is mother's needle

    FiO, FuG

        Craft
        Family
        Hat

1326. This is my book

    HRh, RRR

        Ball
        Book
        Cat
        Rain

1327. This is my eye

    FiO

        Senses
        Touching Rhyme

1328. This is my father

    FFr, LDF

        Counting
        Family
        Feelings

1329. This is my garden

    BPP, FFr, LDF

        Plants and Seeds
        Rain, Sun

1330. This is my house, cozy and neat

    RRR

        Friendship
        Store or Building

1331. This is my little house. This is the door

    GaY

        Smoke
        Store or Building

1332. This is my right hand

    CCO, FFr, FiO,
    FPF, LDF, RRR

        Hand Rhyme
        Left and Right

1333. This is my turtle

    ECT, FPF, LDF,
    RRR

        Animal Home
        In and Out
        Turtle

Index to Fingerplays

1342. This is the family in my household
      FPF
                                    Counting
                                    Family
                                    Growing Up

1343. This is the father, short and stout
      GaY, TLB (m)
                                    Counting
                                    Family
                                    Growing Up
                                    Size

1344. This is the father who brings us our bread
      RFF
                                    Counting
                                    Family
                                    Finger Rhyme

1345. This is the house that I built
      FuG
                                    Store or Building
                                    Tool

1346. This is the house with the sloping roof
      FuG
                                    Cat, Dog
                                    Store or Building
                                    Tree

1347. This is the man that broke the barn
      TPM
                                    Counting
                                    Manners
                                    Scotland

1348. This is the meadow where all the day/ ten little lambs are all at play
      ECT
                                    Counting
                                    Sheep

1349. This is the meadow where all the long day/ ten little frolicsome lambs are at play
      CCO, FiN (m), RRR
                                    Counting
                                    Day and Night
                                    Farmer
                                    Sheep
                                    Store or Building
                                    Winter

1358. This is the squirrel that lives in a tree

    FFr, RFF

                         Animal Home
                         Quiet Time Rhyme
                         Squirrel

1359. This is the sun, high up in the sky

    ECT, RRR

                         Earth and Sky, Plants
                             and Seeds
                         Flower
                         Rain, Sun
                         Up and Down

1360. This is the way, all the long day, the boats go sailing by

    LDF

                         Boat
                         Bridge

1361. This is the way he saws the wood

    FFr

                         Carpenter
                         Tool

1362. This is the way my fingers stand

    LDF, RRR

                         Finger Rhyme
                         Hand Rhyme

1363. This is the way the elephant goes

    FFr, RFF

                         Animal, Elephant,
                             Monkey, Snake

1364. This is the way the flowers sleep

    CCO

                         Flower
                         Plants and Seeds
                         Robin
                         Spring, Winter

1365. This is the way the postman comes walking down the street

    FoD

                         Feelings
                         Left and Right
                         Mail
                         Mail Carrier
                         Senses

1366. This is the way the snow comes down softly, softly falling

      RRR   Flower
                                       Rain, Snow
                                       Spring, Winter

1367. This is the way the snow comes down upon a winter day

      CCO   Snow, Sun
                                       Winter

1368. This is the way these girls and boys can hop and skip and play

      RRR   Friendship
                                       Game
                                       Manners

1369. This is the way we blow our balloons

      ECT, LDF, RRR   Balloon

1370. This is the way we churn the cream

      RRR   Food
                                       Musical Instrument

1371. This is the way we paste our collage

      BPP   Craft

1372. This is the way we wash our clothes

      GaY, LDF, RFF   Chores
                                       Clothes
                                     Months and Days

1373. This is the way we wash our hands

      FFr   Cleanliness

1374. This is the white sheep

      RRR   Craft
                                       Farmer
                                     Sheep

1375. This kitty said, "I smell a mouse"

     CCO

                              Animal Sounds
                              Cat, Mouse
                              Counting
                              Senses

1376. This little bear has a soft fur suit

     CCO, FFr

                              Bear
                              Counting
                              Feelings

1377. This little bird flaps its wings

     TPM

                              Bird

1378. This little boy is ready for bed

     CCO, FiO, FFr,
     FPF, LDF, RFF,
     RRR

                              Bedtime Rhyme
                              Day and Night
                              Religious Rhyme

1379. This little bunny has two pink eyes

     FFr, RFF

                              Counting
                              Rabbit

1380. This little chick ate corn today. This little chick ate worms, they say

     RFF

                              Chicken
                              Counting

1381. This little chick had corn today This little chick had only hay

     FFr

                              Animal Sounds
                              Chicken
                              Counting

1382. This little child brought an egg *(Este ninito compro un huevito)

     *RFF

                              Chile
                              Counting
                              Eggs
                              *Spanish Language Rhyme

1391. This little mountain finds the sun

      RRR

                            Christmas
                            Counting
                            Mountain
                            Tree

1392. This little mousie peeped within

      RRR

                            Counting
                            Mouse
                            Manners

1393. This little mule wants corn

      RRR

                            Animal
                            Counting

1394. This little pig lost his sweater

      FFr

                            Animal Sounds
                            Counting
                            Jack Frost
                            Pig

1395. This little pig makes an "oink, oink, oink"

      RRR

                            Animal Sounds
                            Counting
                            Manners
                            Pig

1396. This little pig wants some corn

      StD (m)

                            Counting
                            Feelings
                            Manners
                            Pig

1397. This little pig went to market

      ADR, CCO, ECT,
      EWT (m), FFr, FiR,
      FPF, FP1, GaY,
      LDF, MuF (m), PAT,
      PBS, RRR, SaG (m),
      StD (m), TeF,
      TLB (m), TNT,
      TPM, TTB

                            Animal Sounds
                            Counting
                            Mother Goose Rhyme
                            Pig

Index to Fingerplays

1406. This mooly cow switched her tail all day

    CCO

                Animal Sounds
                Counting
                Cow

1407. This old man, he played one

    BBP, CCO, EWT (m),
    LDF, PBS, SDG (m),
    TOB (m)

                Counting
                Finger Rhyme
                Hand Rhyme

1408. This one is a little king *(Este es un rey honrado)

    *RFF

                Colombia
                Counting
                *Spanish Language Rhyme

1409. This one's old

    CCO

                Counting

1410. This pig got into the barn

    TNT, TPM

                Animal Sounds
                Counting
                Manners
                Pig

1411. This train is bound for glory

    EWT (m)

                Airplane, Bicycle, Boat,
                  Car, Train
                China
                Fast and Slow
                Feelings

1412. This valentine is for bobble-dee-boo

    CCO

                Counting
                Valentine's Day

1413. Three blind mice

    LiB

                Counting
                Feelings
                Mouse

Index to Fingerplays

1422. Three little oak leaves, red, brown, and gold, were happy when the wind turned cold

      RFF

                                                      Color
Counting
Fall
Tree

1423. Three little pigeons sitting on a fence

      RFF

        Countdown
Feelings
Pigeon

1424. Three little pigs and a little pig more/ knocked on the farmer's bright green door

      GaY

        Addition, Counting
Animal Sounds
Cow, Pig
Farmer
Manners

1425. Three little pumpkins laying very still

      RRR

        Counting
Fruit
Halloween, Thanksgiving

1426. Three mice went into a hole to spin

      TPM

        Cat, Mouse
Counting
Feelings
Safety Rule

1427. Thumb bold

      TPM

        Counting
Finger Rhyme
Scotland

1428. Thumbkin, Pointer, Middleman big

      LDF

        Counting
Finger Rhyme

Index to Fingerplays

1429. Thumbkin says, "I'll dance"

    FFr, FPF, LDF   Counting
                                      Finger Rhyme

1430. Thumbs in the thumb place

    ECT, FPF, GFH,   Finger Rhyme
    LDF, RRR   Mittens
                                        Winter

1431. Tick, tick, tick, tick, says the metronome

    LDF   Fast and Slow
                                      Musical Instrument

1432. Tinker, Tailor, Soldier

    TNT   Counting
                                      Finger Rhyme

1433. A tiny, tiny worm wriggled along like this without a sound

    GaY   Animal
                                      Animal Home

1434. A tired little worm on a cold, stormy day crept out on a branch
    of a tree

    RRR   Animal Home
                                    Butterfly and Caterpillar
                                    Fall, Winter
                                    Snow, Wind

1435. To and fro, to and fro, sweeping with my broom I go

    GaY   Chores

1436. To every friend of mine I'll send a pretty valentine

    FFr, RFF   Counting
                                    Family, Grandparents
                                    Friendship
                                    Valentine's Day

1437. To Grandma's house we go

    FFr
                                 Feelings
                                 Food
                                 Grandparents
                                 Thanksgiving

1438. To see what he could see a little Indian climbed a tree

    FPF
                                 Friendship
                                 Indian
                                 Pilgrim
                                 Thanksgiving

1439. Today I have a birthday

    RFF, RRR, TCB
                                 Birthday
                                 Countdown, Counting
                                 Dessert
                                 Sharing

1440. Today I wore my snow suit

    FFr
                                 Clothes, Hat, Mittens,
                                     Shoes and Boots
                                 Winter

1441. Today is ____'s birthday

    FFr, RFF, RRR,
    TCB
                                 Birthday
                                 Candle
                                 Counting
                                 Dessert

1442. Today was the day for school to begin

    ECT
                                 Friendship
                                 Store or Building

1443. Tommy Thumb, Tommy Tumb, Where are you

    GaY
                                 Counting
                                 Finger Rhyme
                                 Size

1444. Tonight we're having leftovers

    MUD
                                 Food
                                 Hand Rhyme

1453. Turtles are so very slow

    SAP

Fast and Slow
Growing Up
Popcorn
Turtle

1454. Twelve little rabbits in a rabbit pen

    FFr, RFF

Countdown
Rabbit

1455. Twinkle, twinkle, Birthday star

    FPF

Christmas
Religious Rhyme

1456. Twinkle, twinkle, little star, how I wonder what you are

    ADR, GDW (m), ReG,
    SaG (m), TNT

Night Sky

1457. Two candles and two candles, that makes four

    FiO

Addition, Counting
Candle

1458. Two cozy homes stand upon a hill

    LiA

Counting
Day and Night
Quiet Time Rhyme
Store or Building

1459. Two fat gentlemen met in a lane

    ADR, GaY

Counting
Finger Rhyme
Manners
Size

1460. Two hands have I to hold in sight

    CCO

Counting
Hand Rhyme
Left and Right

Index to Fingerplays

1468. Two little ducks that I once knew

      GFH, LDF   Counting
                                          Duck
                                          Size

1469. Two little Easter rabbits resting in the sun

      FFr   Countdown
                                            Easter
                                        Rabbit (Easter)

1470. Two little eyes that open and close

      CCO, FiO   Counting
                                            Open and Shut
                                        Senses
                                        Touching Rhyme

1471. Two little eyes to look around *(Xiao yan-er kan jingzhier)

      GaY, *TLB, TTB   *Chinese Language Rhyme
                                        Counting
                                          Senses
                                        Touching Rhyme

1472. Two little feet go tap, tap, tap

      CCO, ECT, FFr,   Counting
      RRR, TCB   Quiet Time Rhyme

1473. Two little friends are better than one

      RRR, TCB   Counting
                                          Friendship
                                        Sharing

1474. Two little hands so clean and bright

      FPF   Counting
                                        Hand Rhyme
                                        Left and Right

1475. Two little hands so soft and white

      JTJ, LDF   Counting
                                          Hand Rhyme
                                        Left and Right

1476. Two little houses closed up tight

        CCO, FFr, LDF,   Counting
        RFF, RRR   Open and Shut
                                      Store or Building
                                      Telling Time

1477. Two little monkeys fighting in bed

        FFr, HRh, RRR   Counting
                                        Manners
                                        Monkey

1478. Two little monkeys sitting in a tree

        FPF   Addition, Counting
                                        Monkey
                                        Tree

1479. Two little puppets, one on each hand

        LiB, RRR   Counting
                                          Toy

1480. Two little puppy dogs lying in a heap

        CCO   Animal Sounds
                                        Cat, Dog
                                        Counting
                                        Manners

1481. Two merry blue eyes, a cute little nose

        FiO   Christmas
                                        Counting
                                        Santa Claus
                                        Touching Rhyme

1482. Two mother pigs lived in a pen

        FFr, LDF, PBS,   Addition
        RRR   Pig
                                        Counting

1483. Two small hands that touch in prayer

        RFF   Christmas
                                        Counting
                                        Religious Rhyme

1484. Two tall telephone poles, between them a wire is strung

    RFF, RRR

        Bird
        Counting
        Structure

1485. Two twin airplanes flying high

    MuG (m)

        Airplane
        Counting
        Safety Rule

1486. Two wheels, three wheels on the ground

    ECT

        Bicycle
        Counting

1487. The typewriter is a funny machine

    FuG

        Machine

U

1488. Under a stone where the earth was firm

    GaY

        Animal
        Animal Home

1489. Under a toadstool there sat a wee elf

    RFF

        Counting
        Craft
        Fairy or Giant
        Feelings

1490. Under the spreading chestnut tree

    CCO

        Feelings
        Touching Rhyme
        Tree

Index to Fingerplays

1491. United States has a birthday

      FPF
                    Fourth of July
                                Months and Days
                                Musical Instrument
                                United States

1492. Up a step, and up a step, and up a step, and up

      LDF
                    Playground
                    Structure

1493. Up and down, and round and round

      FFr
                    Health
                    Up and Down

1494. Up from the ground with a whir and a roar

      SAP
                    Airplane
                    Up and Down

1495. Up in a tree is a little bird's nest

      GFH
                    Animal Home
                    Bird
                    Counting

1496. Up on the housetop reindeers pause

      BPP
                    Christmas
                    Feelings
                    Reindeer (Santa's)
                    Santa Claus

1497. Up the candlestick he ran

      CCO, GaY
                Mouse
                Up and Down

1498. Up the hill—down the hill

      RRR
                    Counting
                    Hand Rhyme
                    High and Low, Up
                      and Down

1499. Up the steps we will go

      LDF

Door or Steps
Fast and Slow, Up
   and Down
Playground

1500. Upon each hand a little band for work or play is ready

      CCO

Counting
Size

1501. Use your ears

      ECT

Guessing Rhyme
Senses

1502. Use your eyes

      ECT, RRR

Color
Senses
Shoes and Boots

V

1503. A valentine for you

      LDF

Friendship
Valentine's Day

1504. The valentine Dad gave to Mom

      CCO

Family
Food
Valentine's Day

1505. Valentines, valentines; how many do you see

      FFr, RFF

Counting
Family
Sharing
Valentine's Day

1506. Valentines, valentines: red, white, and blue

      RRR, TCB

                    Color
                    Sharing
                    Valentine's Day

1507. A very old witch was stirring a pot

      LiA

                    Ghost or Goblin
                    Halloween
                    Witch

W

1508. Waddle E Ah Cha

      RRR

                    Copy Cat Rhyme

1509. Waddle, waddle, waddle duck

      CCO

                    Duck
                    Up and Down

1510. Wake up, little fingers, the morning has come

      RFF, RRR

                    Hand Rhyme

1511. Wake up little pilgrims, the sun's in the east

      FFr, RFF

                    Cleanliness
                    Directions
                    Pilgrim
                    Religious Rhyme
                    Thanksgiving

1512. Warm hands, warm

      FFr, LDF, TLB (m)

                    Concept
                    Hand Rhyme

1513. The watch on my arm makes a little click

      CCO

                    Clock or Watch
                    Senses

1514. The waves rise high

    SAP   Sea and Seashore

1515. Way up high in an apple tree, one little apple smiled down at me

    BPP, CCO, ECT,   Apple Tree
    FPF, FP2, GFH,   Counting
    LDF, TCB   Fruit
                                           Up and Down

1516. We are going to plant a bean

    BPP, GaY   Feelings
                                           Plants and Seeds
                                           Summer, Winter
                                           Sun, Wind

1517. We are ten little snowflakes floating to the ground

    FoD   Bedtime Rhyme
                                           Counting
                                           Fairy or Giant
                                           Snow
                                           Winter

1518. We are woodmen sawing trees

    GaY   Career
                                           Tool
                                           Tree

1519. We have a pumpkin, a big orange pumpkin

    FFr   Halloween
                                           Jack-o-Lantern

1520. We made a snowman in our yard

    FFr   Snowman
                                           Winter

1521. We sat around the campfire on a chilly night

    ECT   Bedtime Rhyme
                                           Concept
                                           Halloween
                                           Sports or Hobbies

1530. We're going on a shopping trip

RRR   Store or Building

1531. We're going to pick blueberries

MUD   Dessert, Fruit

1532. We're growing a little garden here

MUD   Plants and Seeds
                                       Up and Down
                                       Vegetable

1533. We'll hop, hop, hop like a bunny

FFr, RFF   Bird
                                       Dog, Elephant, Fish, Frog
                                         or Toad, Rabbit
                                       Quiet Time Rhyme

1534. What can you do, Punchinello, funny fellow

RRR   Copy Cat Rhyme

1535. What do you suppose? A bee sat on my nose

ADR, BBP, FPF,   Bee
GaY   Manners

1536. What does little birdie say in her nest at peek of day

FFr   Bird
                                       Growing Up

1537. What does the clock in the hall say

GaY   Clock or Watch

1538. "What makes you run, my little man, you are all out of breath"

FFr   Halloween
                                       Jack-o-Lantern

1539. What shall we do with the baby-o

EWT (m), MuF (m)   Baby, Family
                                       Bird
                                       Frog or Toad
                                       Wind

Index to Fingerplays

1540. What's fluffy-white and floats up high

        ECT, RRR   Earth and Sky
                                             Guessing Rhyme

1541. What's that sitting on the fence up there

        FFr   Cat
                                             Guessing Rhyme
                                             Halloween
                                           Jack-o-Lantern

1542. The wheels on the bus go round and round

        ADR, BPP, ECT,   Bus
        EWT (m), GaY,   Up and Down
        LDF, PBS, PRh (m),
        RRR, Sta, TCB,
        TNT, TOB (m),
        WAA (m)

1543. When a little chicken eats, he scampers all around

        RRR   Chicken
                                             Up and Down

1544. When a robin cocks its head

        RRR, TCB   Animal
                                               Robin
                                             Senses

1545. When a yellow duck walks down the street

        RRR   Animal Sounds
                                             Duck

1546. When all the cows were sleeping

        GaY, GFH   Fall
                                               Halloween
                                             Night Sky
                                           Scarecrow

1547. When cold winds blow

      ECT, RRR, TCB
                                      Bedtime Rhyme
                                      Concept
                                      Snow, Wind
                                      Winter

1548. When Daddy washes our automobile

      SAP
                                        Car
                                      Chores
                                      Family
                                      Helping Others

1549. When goblins prowl

      RRR
                                        Animal Sounds
                                        Feelings
                                        Ghost or Goblin
                                        Halloween
                                        Owl
                                        Witch

1550. When Granddad reads the paper

      SAP
                                        Grandparents
                                        Size

1551. When I come in from outdoor play

      ECT, RRR
                                        Clothes
                                      Feelings
                                      Helping Others
                                        Winter

1552. When I get ready to come to Story Hour

      RRR
                                        Cleanliness, Health
                                      Dressing
                                      Feelings
                                      Food

1553. When I grow up, I'll say "Good-bye"

      RRR
                                        Airplane, Boat, Car, Train

1564. When Santa comes down the chimney

    FFr

    Bedtime Rhyme
Christmas
Santa Claus

1565. When story hour morning rolls around

    RRR

    Concept
Growing Up

1566. When the hands on the clock show it is time for bed

    FoD

    Bedtime Rhyme
Cleanliness
Telling Time

1567. When the leaves are on the ground

    FFr

    Fall
Senses
Tree

1568. When the farmer's day is done

    CCO

    Animal Sounds
Counting
Day and Night
Farmer
Manners

1569. When the siren blows

    ECT

    Safety Rule

1570. When the sun lights up the sky

    RRR

    Dressing
Earth and Sky
Health
Sun

1571. When we go to the county fair

    MUD

    Food
Circus or Carnival

Index to Fingerplays

1580. The whistle blows at the factory

    ECT

        Career
        Store or Building

1581. White feathered magpie *(Soroka-beloboka)

    *TLB (m)

        Bird
        Counting
        Food
        *Russian Language Rhyme
        Tickling Rhyme

1582. White sheep, white sheep, on a blue hill

    Sta

        Guessing Rhyme
        Sheep

1583. Who comes creeping in the night when the moon is clear and bright

    RRR

        Color
        Fall
        Guessing Rhyme
        In and Out, Up and Down
        Jack Frost
        Tree

1584. Who feels happy, who feels gay

    ECT, JTJ, LDF,
    RRR, TCB

        Copy Cat Rhyme
        Feelings

1585. Who is coming down the chimney tonight

    CCO

        Christmas
        Feelings
        Santa Claus

1586. Who is it that wears a happy smile

    RRR

        Clown
        Feelings
        Guessing Rhyme

1587. "Who stole the cookie from the cookie jar"

    FP2, RRR, TOB (m)

        Dessert
        Feelings
        Guessing Rhyme

Index to Fingerplays

1588. Who's that tapping at my window

        RRR, SDG (m)   Friendship
                                         Guessing Rhyme
                                         Manners

1589. "Who's that tickling my back?" said the wall

        TLB (m)   Butterfly and Caterpillar
                                         Tickling Rhyme

1590. Wiggle, wiggle, fingers right up to the sky

        RRR   Finger Rhyme

1591. Will you have a cookie

        RRR   Dessert, Food
                                         Manners
                                       Sharing

1592. Will you wear white

        EWT (m), RRR   Clothes
                                         Color
                                       Hand Rhyme

1593. Willum he had seven sons

        GaY   Chores
                                       Copy Cat Rhyme
                                       Counting

1594. The wind came out to play one day

        ECT, FFr, FiO,   Wind
        RFF, RRR

1595. The wind is full of tricks today

        ECT, RRR, TCB   April Fools 'Day
                                       Senses
                                       Wind

1596. Wind the bobbin up

        GaY   Counting
                                       Craft

1597. Wind the top

      RRR   Fast and Slow
                                             Top

1598. Wind, wind, wind the bobbin

      LDF   Craft

1599. The winds of March begin to blow

      FFr, RFF   Craft
                                             Kite
                                             Months and Days
                                             Spring
                                             Wind

1600. The windshield wipers on our car are busy in the rain

      LDF, RRR   Car
                                             Fast and Slow, Up
                                                  and Down
                                             Rain

1601. Winking, blinking, see that little light

      CCO   Insect

1602. Winkum—jump up

      RRR   Up and Down

1603. A witch, she went a-shopping one October day

      RRR   Chores
                                             Day and Night
                                             Dressing
                                             Halloween
                                             Months and Days
                                             Telling Time
                                             Witch

1604. Witch, old witch, how do you fly

      CCO   Counting
                                             Halloween
                                             Witch

Index to Fingerplays

1614. Wooden soldiers, red and blue

        RRR, TCB   Musical Instrument
                                          Toy Soldier

1615. Worms and germs and rainy days

        ECT   Nature
                                          Sports or Hobbies

1616. Would you like a cookie

        GFH   Dessert, Food
                                          Manners
                                          Sharing

Y

1617. The yellow giraffe is as tall as can be

        ECT, FFr   Animal
                                          Size

1618. Yellow kernels we will take

        CCO   Popcorn

1619. You and me, we're gonna be partners

        DEH (m)   Feelings
                                          Friendship
                                          Pat-a-Cake Rhyme

1620. You are my friend

        LAL   Feelings
                                          Friendship
                                          Religious Rhyme

1621. You can take your dirty clothes and throw them in the tub

        ECT   Chores
                                          Cleanliness
                                          Clothes
                                        Machine

Z

BIBLIOGRAPHY

ADR—A DAY OF RHYMES selected and illustrated by Sarah Pooley. New York: Alfred A. Knopf, 1987.

BFG—BOOK OF 1000 FAMILY GAMES by The Reader's Digest Association, Inc. Pleasantville, New York: The Reader's Digest Association, Inc., 1971.

BPP—BOOKSHARING: 101 PROGRAMS TO USE WITH PRESCHOOLERS by Margaret Read MacDonald. Illustrated by Julie Liana MacDonald. Hamden, Connecticut: Library Professional Publications, 1988.

CCh—CHANTS FOR CHILDREN compiled by M. L. Colgin. Illustrated by Jim Harter. Manlius, New York: Colgin Publishing, 1982.

CCC—CHILDREN ARE CHILDREN ARE CHILDREN: AN ACTIVITY APPROACH TO EXPLORING BRAZIL, FRANCE, IRAN, JAPAN, NIGERIA AND THE USSR by Ann Cole, Carolyn Haas, Elizabeth Heller, and Betty Weinberger. Illustrated by Lois Axeman. Boston: Little, Brown and Company, 1978.

CCO—CHILDREN'S COUNTING-OUT RHYMES, FINGERPLAYS, JUMP-ROPE AND BOUNCE-BALL CHANTS AND OTHER RHYTHMS compiled and written by Gloria T. Delamar. Jefferson, North Carolina: McFarland, 1983.

DEH—DO YOUR EARS HANG LOW? FIFTY MORE MUSICAL FINGERPLAYS by Tom Glazer. Illustrated by Mila Lazarevich. Garden City, New York: Doubleday & Company, Inc., 1980.

ECT—EVERYDAY CIRCLE TIMES by Liz and Dick Wilmes. Illustrated by Jeane Healy. Dundee, Illinois: Building Blocks, 1983.

EWT—EYE WINKER TOM TINKER CHIN CHOPPER: FIFTY MUSICAL FINGERPLAYS by Tom Glazer. Illustrated by Ron Himler. Garden City, New York: Doubleday & Company, Inc., 1973.

Index to Fingerplays

FFr—FINGER FROLICS compiled by Liz Cromwell and Dixie Hibner. Edited by John R. Faitel. Illustrated by Sue Yagiela Williams. Livonia, Michigan: Partner Press, 1976.

FFu—FINGER FUN, SONGS AND RHYTHMS FOR THE VERY YOUNG by Helen Wright Salisbury. Photography by Robert Thomsen. Los Angeles: Cowman Publications, Inc., 1955.

FiN—FINGER PLAYS FOR NURSERY AND KINDERGARTEN, by Emilie Poulsson. Illustrated by L. J. Bridgman. Music by Cornelia C. Roeske. New York: Dover Publications, Inc., 1971. (Originally published by D. Lothrop and Company, Boston, 1893.)

FiO—FINGER PLAYS THAT MOTIVATE: A COLLECTION OF TESTED AND NOVEL ACTION VERSES by Don Peck. Minneapolis: T. S. Denison and Company, Inc., 1975.

FiP—FINGER PUPPETS: EASY TO MAKE, FUN TO USE by Laura Ross. Illustrated by Laura and Frank Ross, Jr. New York: Lothrop, Lee, and Shepard Company, 1971.

FiR—FINGER RHYMES collected and illustrated by Marc Brown. New York: E. P. Dutton, 1980.

FMa—FINGERMATH, Book 1, TEACHERS EDITION by Peter K. Gurau and Edwin M. Lieberthal. New York: McGraw-Hill Book Company, 1977.

FoD—FINGERPLAY APPROACH TO DRAMATIZATION by Mary Jackson Ellis. Illustrated by Carvel Lee. Minneapolis: T. T. Denison & Co., Inc., 1960.

FPF—FINGERPLAY FRIENDS: ACTION RHYMES FOR HOME, CHURCH, AND SCHOOL by Audrey Olson Leighton. Valley Forge, Pennsylvania: Judson Press, 1984.

FP1—FINGERPLAYS AND ACTION CHANTS, VOLUME ONE: ANIMALS by Tonja Evetts Weimer. Illustrated by Yvonne Kozlina. Pittsburgh: Pearce-Evetts Publishing, 1986.

FP2—FINGERPLAYS AND ACTION CHANTS, VOLUME TWO: FAMILY AND FRIENDS by Tonja Evetts Weimer. Illustrated by Yvonne Kozlina. Pittsburgh: Pearce-Evetts Publishing, 1986.

FPH—FINGERPUPPETS, FINGERPLAYS AND HOLIDAYS by Betty Keefe.

Photographs by Connie Champlin. Omaha, Nebraska: Special Literature Press, 1984.

FuG—FUN AND GAMES by Margaret E. Mulac. Illustrated by Julianne. New York: Harper & Brothers, 1956.

GaY—GAMES FOR THE VERY YOUNG: FINGER PLAYS AND NURSERY GAMES compiled by Elizabeth Matterson. Illustrated by Raymond Briggs and David Woodroffe. New York: American Heritage Press, 1969. (Originally published as THIS LITTLE PUFFIN. Harmondsworth, Middlesex: Penguin Books Limited, 1969.)

GDW—GO IN AND OUT THE WINDOW: AN ILLUSTRATED SONGBOOK FOR YOUNG PEOPLE edited by Dan Fox. New York: Henry Holt and Company/The Metropolitan Museum of Art, 1987.

GFH—GOING ON A FINGER PLAY HUNT edited by Cynthia Percak Infantino. Wheeling, Illinois: Children's Librarians Unit/Regional Library Advisory Council, 1977.

HRh—HAND RHYMES collected and illustrated by Marc Brown. New York: E. P. Dutton, 1985.

JTJ—JUBA THIS AND JUBA THAT: STORY HOUR STRETCHES FOR LARGE OR SMALL GROUPS selected by Virginia A. Tashjian. Illustrated by Victoria de Larrea. Boston: Little, Brown and Company, 1969.

LAL—LEARNING ABOUT LIVING: KINDERGARTEN by Ruth Lewis Camburn and Carole Matthews. Edited by Lila Bishop. Designed by Scot A. McDonald. Wheaton, Illinois: Pioneer Clubs, 1987.

LDF—LET'S DO FINGERPLAYS by Marion Grayson. Illustrated by Nancy Weyl. Washington: Robert B. Luce, Inc., 1962.

LiA—LISTEN! AND HELP TELL THE STORY by Bernice Wells Carlson. Illustrated by Burmah Burris. Nashville: Abingdon Press, 1965.

LiB—LITTLE BOY BLUE: FINGER PLAYS OLD AND NEW by Daphne Hogstrom. Illustrated by Alice Schlesinger. Racine, Wisconsin: Golden Press, Western Publishing Company, Inc., 1966.

MiM—MITT MAGIC: FINGERPLAYS FOR FINGER PUPPETS by Lynda Roberts. Illustrated by James Morris. Mt. Rainier, Maryland: Gryphon House Inc., 1985.

MUD—MUDLUSCIOUS: STORIES AND ACTIVITIES FEATURING FOOD FOR PRESCHOOL CHILDREN by Jan Irving and Robin Currie. Illustrated by Robert B. Phillips. Littleton, Colorado: Libraries Unlimited, Inc., 1986.

MuF—MUSIC FOR ONES AND TWOS: SONGS AND GAMES FOR THE VERY YOUNG CHILD by Tom Glazer. Illustrated by Karen Ann Weinhaus. Garden City, New York: Doubleday & Company, Inc., 1983.

MuG—MUSICAL GAMES FOR CHILDREN OF ALL AGES by Esther L. Nelson. Illustrated by Shizu Matsuda. New York: Sterling Publishing Co., Inc., 1976.

MyB—MY BIG BOOK OF FINGER PLAYS: A FUN-TO-SAY, FUN-TO-PLAY COLLECTION by Daphne Hogstrom. Illustrated by Sally Augustiny. Racine, Wisconsin: Golden Press, Western Publishing Company, Inc., 1974.

PaR—PARTY RHYMES, collected and illustrated by Marc Brown. New York: E. P. Dutton, 1988.

PAT—PAT-A-CAKE AND OTHER GAMES FOR BABY. Illustrated by Dan Siculan. Chicago: Rand McNally & Company, 1970.

PBS—PICTURE BOOK STORY HOURS FROM BIRTHDAYS TO BEARS by Paula Gaj Sitarz. Littleton, Colorado: Libraries Unlimited, Inc., 1987.

PRh—PLAY RHYMES collected and illustrated by Marc Brown. New York: E. P. Dutton, 1987.

ReG—RECREATION LEADER'S GUIDE by Myrtle Edwards. Illustrated by Janet Nakaji. Palo Alto, California: National Press Books, 1967.

RFF—RHYMES FOR FINGERS AND FLANNELBOARDS by Louise Binder Scott and J. J. Thompson. Illustrated by Jean Flowers. St. Louis, Missouri: McGraw-Hill Book Company, Webster Division, 1960.

RRR—RING A RING O'ROSES: STORIES, GAMES AND FINGER PLAYS FOR PRE-SCHOOL CHILDREN by Flint Public Library. Flint, Michigan: The Flint Board of Education, 1981.

SaG—SALLY GO: THREE HUNDRED CHILDREN'S SONGS, RHYMES AND GAMES collected and edited by Edith Fowke. Illustrated by Carlos Marchiori. Musical arrangements by Keith MacMillan. Garden City, New York: Doubleday & Company, Inc., 1978.

SAP—SAY IT AND PLAY IT: FIFTY-TWO ACTION PLAYS FOR CHILDREN by Edith M. Leonard and Dorothy D. VanDeman. Evanston, Illinois: Row, Peterson and Company, 1950.

SDG—SINGING AND DANCING GAMES FOR THE VERY YOUNG by Esther L. Nelson. Illustrated by Minn Matsuda. Photographs by Shirley Zeiberg. New York: Sterling Publishing Company, Inc., 1980.

SmC—SMALL WORLD CELEBRATIONS by Jean Warren and Elizabeth McKinnon. Illustrated by Marion Hopping Ekberg. Everett, Washington: Warren Publishing House, Inc., 1988.

Sta—STAMP YOUR FEET ACTION RHYMES selected by Sarah Hayes. Illustrated by Toni Goffe. New York: Lothrop, Lee & Shepard Books, 1988.

StD—STEP IT DOWN: GAMES, PLAYS, SONGS, AND STORIES FROM THE AFRO-AMERICAN HERITAGE by Bessie Jones and Bess Lomax Hawes. New York: Harper & Row, 1972.

TCB—THE CIRCLE TIME BOOK: FOR HOLIDAYS AND SPECIAL OCCUR-RENCES THROUGHOUT THE YEAR by Liz and Dick Wilmes. Illustrated by Donna Dane. Dundee, Illinois: Building Blocks, 1982.

TeF—TEN LITTLE FINGERS TEN LITTLE TOES: NURSERY GAMES AND FINGER PLAYS FOR THE VERY YOUNG. Illustrated by Vivienne DeMuth. New York: Gingerbread House, 1979.

TLB—THE LAUGHING BABY: REMEMBERING NURSERY RHYMES AND REASONS by Anne Scott. Illustrated by Lura Schwarz Smith. Musical score calligraphy by Donna Dee Politi. South Hadley, Massachusetts: Bergin & Garvey Publishers, Inc., 1987.

TNT—THE NURSERY TREASURY: A COLLECTION OF BABY GAMES, RHYMES AND LULLABIES selected by Sally Emerson. Illustrated by Moira and Colin Maclean. New York: Doubleday & Company, Inc., 1988.

TOB—THE WHEELS OF THE BUS GO ROUND AND ROUND: SCHOOL BUS SONGS AND CHANTS collected by Nancy Larrick. Illustrated by Gene Holtan. Music arranged by Patty Zeitlin. San Carlos, California: Golden Gate Junior Books, 1972.

TPM—THIS LITTLE PIG WENT TO MARKET compiled by Norah Montgomerie. Illustrated by Margery Gill. New York: Franklin Watts, Inc., 1966.

TTB—TROT TROT TO BOSTON: PLAY RHYMES FOR BABY compiled by

Carol F. Ra. Illustrated by Catherine Stock. New York: William Morrow & Company, Lothrop, Lee & Shepard Books Division, —1987.

UBC—UNICEF BOOK OF CHILDREN'S SONGS compiled by William I. Kaufman. Photographs by the author. Musical arrangements by Denes Agay. English lyrics by Joan Gilbert Van Poznak. Harrisburg, Pennsylvania: Stackpole Books, 1970.

WAA—WHAT SHALL WE DO AND ALLEE GALLOO! PLAY SONGS AND SINGING GAMES FOR YOUNG CHILDREN collected and edited by Marie Winn. Illustrated by Karla Kuskin. Musical arrangements by Allan Miller. New York: Harper & Row, 1970.

WAI—WHO AM I? ACTIVITY SONGS FOR YOUNG CHILDREN by Lois Raebeck. Illustrated by June Goldsborough. Chicago: Follett Publishing Company, 1970.

WDS—WITH A DEEP SEA SMILE: STORY HOUR STRETCHES FOR LARGE AND SMALL GROUPS selected by Virginia A. Tashjian. Illustrated by Rosemary Wells. Boston: Little, Brown and Company, Inc., 1974.

PART
II

SUBJECT
INDEXES

INDEX BY SUBJECT

Fingerplay subjects are listed below alphabetically. The numbers that follow each individual entry refer you to the corresponding entry number from this book's Main Index.

ANIMALS

Alligator (or Crocodile)

Bear

Cat

Cow

Dinosaur

Index to Fingerplays

Dog

73, 75, 146, 285, 309-10, 378, 448, 556, 558, 570, 586, 639, 651, 688, 743, 784, 802, 812, 866, 955, 958, 964, 981, 1029, 1070, 1114, 1168, 1274, 1278, 1314, 1346, 1385, 1400, 1480, 1533

Elephant

17, 77, 175-77, 234, 257, 378, 433, 530, 639, 651, 956, 975, 991, 1093, 1216, 1363, 1533, 1607

Fish

75, 211, 260-61, 362, 379, 476, 575, 583, 776, 786, 790, 817, 865, 1009, 1168, 1204, 1238-39, 1271, 1533, 1554, 1629

Frog or Toad

75, 140, 264-67, 327, 370, 442, 501, 513, 523-24, 613, 788, 790, 958, 1006, 1031, 1240, 1295, 1387, 1418-19, 1533, 1539

Giraffe

17, 639

Horse

223, 277, 305, 547, 586, 592, 638, 688, 703, 859, 920, 924, 928, 1154, 1221, 1253

Kangaroo

64, 639, 727, 991, 1124

Lion

17, 378, 651, 761, 991, 1216

Monkey

3, 17, 159, 295-97, 378, 553-54, 651, 758, 797, 847, 982, 991, 1027, 1216, 1363, 1420-21, 1477-78

Mouse

77, 122, 291-93, 298, 312, 444, 469, 507, 579, 676, 798-99, 803, 818, 855, 858, 900, 1112, 1116, 1141, 1172, 1182, 1238, 1284, 1287, 1296, 1321, 1375, 1392, 1413, 1426, 1497, 1572

Pig

38, 131, 205, 303, 463, 547, 638, 688, 705, 745, 802, 924, 1048-49, 1303, 1394-97, 1410, 1424, 1482

Rabbit

67, 70, 75, 95, 118, 123, 185, 189, 313, 378, 430,433, 438, 447, 449, 464, 570, 607, 609, 613, 639, 756, 776, 779, 781, 801, 803, 814, 862, 881, 887,908, 927, 942, 945, 958, 1029, 1077, 1079-80, 1098, 1120, 1142, 1183, 1225-27, 1256, 1273, 1277, 1282, 1306, 1311, 1379, 1402, 1454, 1465, 1533

Rabbit (Easter)

162-65, 168-69, 225, 242, 256, 610, 678, 933, 1078, 1305, 1469

Reindeer (Santa's)

93, 174, 315, 466, 503, 630, 904, 1012, 1496

Sheep

146, 463, 504, 547, 688, 770-71, 802, 812, 964, 1348-49, 1357, 1374, 1582

Skunk

616, 1089, 1629

Snail

638, 808, 1166, 1172, 1174, 1322

Snake

149, 159, 433, 474, 611, 666, 1295, 1363

Index to Fingerplays

Spider

171, 474, 575, 586, 653, 796, 956, 1341

Squirrel

328-30, 394, 665, 696, 744, 756, 791, 809, 1013, 1194, 1263, 1272, 1291, 1297, 1358, 1366, 1403, 1579

Tiger

758, 975, 991, 1404

Turtle

433, 950, 978, 1285, 1333, 1453

Additional Animals

3, 77, 273, 275, 366, 378, 403, 474, 518, 639, 668, 681-82, 810, 818, 975, 991, 1010, 1073, 1080, 1089, 1114, 1133, 1157, 1168, 1216, 1363, 1393, 1415, 1433, 1488, 1544, 1617

See also: **Animal Homes** and **Animal Sounds** under *Nature*

ART

Color

10, 21, 137, 141, 156, 163, 233, 255, 287, 290, 323, 398, 421, 500, 738, 795, 820, 824, 848, 930, 933, 1071, 1084, 1089, 1090, 1139, 1206, 1271, 1305, 1422, 1502, 1506, 1574, 1583, 1592

Craft

419, 582, 702, 860, 883, 1176, 1287, 1325, 1357, 1371, 1374, 1489, 1596, 1598-99

Shape

59, 110, 152-55, 160-61, 183, 488, 497, 505, 713, 816, 876, 931, 1104, 1143

See also: **Jack-o-Lantern** under **Halloween** in *Holidays and Birthdays*

BEDTIME RHYMES

15, 39, 67, 82, 107, 117-18, 124, 221, 238, 331, 372, 447, 460, 474, 502, 504, 508, 519, 532, 635, 676, 705, 726, 768, 782, 862, 871, 886, 898, 901, 1019, 1094, 1126, 1204, 1213-14, 1290, 1307, 1312, 1315, 1378, 1389, 1416, 1517, 1521, 1527, 1547, 1564, 1566, 1610

BIRDS

Blackbird

83, 360, 1162, 1292, 1463-64

Chickadee

245, 1229, 1417

Chicken

72, 117, 188, 226, 246, 386, 420, 463, 478-80, 504, 515, 547, 558, 570, 617, 638, 688, 851, 924, 964, 1019, 1044, 1122, 1154, 1380-81, 1452, 1466, 1543

Crow

341, 929, 964, 1075, 1279, 1414

Duck

75, 146, 251-54, 412, 513, 547, 558, 570, 613, 631, 654, 688, 836, 924, 1164-65, 1220, 1231-32, 1295, 1452, 1468, 1509, 1545

Goose

90, 496, 547, 631, 837, 974, 1452

Owl

298, 413, 450, 474, 498, 774, 838, 1034-35, 1452,1549

Index to Fingerplays

Penguin

991, 994, 1250

Pigeon

688, 857, 886, 1251, 1423

Robin

201, 316, 449, 634, 804-06, 1099, 1364, 1452, 1544

Sparrow

325-26, 776, 780

Turkey

213, 228-30, 333-35, 359, 374, 455, 600, 749, 775, 836, 1028, 1208, 1218, 1269, 1450-52

Wren

13, 281, 720

Additional Birds

40, 48-49, 75, 82, 159, 190, 211, 241, 319, 372, 429, 452, 459, 473-74, 508, 547, 572, 586, 597, 602, 606, 634-35, 639, 696, 740, 756, 783, 802, 943, 958, 972, 1089, 1204, 1208, 1212, 1224, 1238, 1288, 1304, 1311, 1377, 1452, 1462, 1467, 1484, 1495, 1524, 1533, 1536, 1539, 1581, 1613

CLOTHING AND DRESSING

Costume

130, 375, 499, 649, 1528

Dressing

85, 271, 411, 538, 669, 677, 757, 892, 1270, 1389, 1552, 1570, 1603

CONCEPTS AND LEARNING SKILLS

Index to Fingerplays

Hand Rhyme

Money

Months and Days

Peace

Quiet Time Rhyme

Safety Rule

Senses

Size

1136-37, 1164-65, 1177, 1185, 1190, 1196, 1275, 1281, 1289, 1302, 1323-24, 1343, 1350-52, 1383, 1443, 1452, 1459, 1461, 1468, 1500, 1523, 1550, 1617

Spelling Rhyme

72, 215, 905, 1014, 1278

Telling Time

113, 180, 271, 507, 562, 565, 988, 1226, 1476, 1527, 1566, 1603, 1606

Clock or Watch

45, 507, 562, 565, 1513, 1537, 1606

Touching Rhyme

26, 63, 100, 116, 128, 181-82, 184, 231, 393, 408-09, 414-16, 426-27, 430, 433, 478-80, 537, 539, 574, 576, 596, 601, 618-19, 650, 671-72, 709, 719, 730-31, 785, 822, 875, 885, 896, 902, 920, 936, 990, 1074, 1076, 1081, 1087, 1094, 1096, 1104, 1112-14, 1156, 1213, 1315, 1327, 1339, 1447, 1461, 1470-71, 1481, 1490

Additional Concepts and Skills

178, 664, 1512, 1521, 1547, 1562, 1565

See also: **Math** and **Opposites**

COUNTRIES

Australia

681, 733

Brazil

891

Chile

891, 1120, 1382

Index to Fingerplays

FAMILY LIFE

Baby

Family

Grandparents

FLOWERS

Daisy

Rose

Additional Flowers

See also: **Plants** and **Seeds** under *Nature*

FOODS AND EATING

Bread

30, 32, 59, 120, 147, 186-87, 224, 249, 301, 488, 505, 511, 749, 830, 910, 1162, 1169, 1622

Dessert

32, 94, 120, 219, 243, 391, 404, 418, 531, 695, 704, 749, 792, 844, 861, 869, 1037, 1059, 1103, 1158, 1162-63, 1228, 1287, 1336, 1340, 1439, 1441, 1531, 1587, 1591, 1616, 1625

Eggs

166, 226, 255, 471, 515, 517, 933, 1068, 1305, 1382

Fruit

10, 23, 30, 120-21, 126, 306-08, 342, 345-46, 348, 405, 450, 454, 491, 549, 642, 701, 792, 816, 926, 931, 946, 1017, 1021, 1046, 1069, 1084, 1089, 1139, 1254, 1265-66, 1336, 1399, 1425, 1515, 1525, 1531

Kitchen Utensils or Dishes

139, 425, 487, 536, 661, 912, 1005, 1060, 1064, 1222, 1340, 1611, 1627

Pancakes

28, 351, 697, 843

Popcorn

525, 1062-63, 1161, 1205, 1453, 1618

Vegetable

76, 89, 95, 121, 131, 142, 207, 299, 543, 567, 746, 894, 927, 942, 945, 1029, 1139, 1176, 1207, 1532

Index to Fingerplays

Additional Games

56, 435, 486, 512, 604, 724, 797, 866, 873, 877, 1368

HEALTH, EMOTIONS, AND BEHAVIOR

Chores

22, 65, 68, 73, 139, 258, 469, 482, 493-94, 512, 580-81, 589, 644, 722, 736, 853, 948, 953, 986, 1186, 1202, 1270, 1341, 1372, 1435, 1548, 1593, 1603, 1610, 1621

Cleanliness

1, 27, 107, 138, 203, 418, 512, 532, 538, 584, 873, 953, 1270, 1373, 1511, 1552, 1566, 1621

Feelings

46, 91-92, 108, 129-30, 132, 165, 167, 264-65, 268-69, 274, 289-90, 313, 321, 347, 357, 359, 380, 392, 410, 445, 527, 554, 582, 594, 596, 605, 612, 626, 628, 658, 663, 674, 760, 762, 814, 818, 867, 874, 904, 948, 957, 960, 972-73, 985, 1006, 1049, 1078, 1134, 1152, 1173, 1192, 1219, 1250, 1269, 1295, 1322, 1328, 1336, 1350, 1353, 1365, 1376, 1384-85, 1387, 1396, 1398, 1411, 1413, 1423, 1426, 1437, 1461, 1463, 1465, 1489-90, 1496, 1516, 1528, 1549, 1551-52, 1554, 1584-87, 1619-20, 1629

Friendship

59, 264-65, 274, 290, 301, 364, 380, 424, 447, 531, 577, 604, 612, 624, 674, 718, 773, 787, 827, 866, 872, 906, 955, 958, 982, 1058, 1127, 1145, 1180, 1275, 1288, 1298, 1330, 1368, 1435, 1436, 1438, 1442, 1473, 1503, 1588, 1619-20, 1627

Growing Up

231, 355, 599, 622, 672, 990, 1342-43, 1350, 1453, 1536, 1560, 1565

Helping Others

68, 73, 119, 139, 235, 343, 371, 422, 445, 512, 580-81, 589, 626, 644, 870, 948, 953, 1058, 1152, 1270, 1314, 1388, 1548, 1551

Index to Fingerplays

Manners

360, 392, 487, 553, 688, 808, 841, 867, 874, 885, 893, 973, 1048, 1136, 1152, 1189, 1219, 1241, 1347, 1368, 1372, 1388, 1392, 1395-96, 1410, 1418, 1424, 1459, 1461, 1477, 1480, 1529, 1535, 1568, 1588, 1591, 1616

Remembering

585, 923, 1061

Sharing

106, 235, 290, 392, 421, 487, 531, 604, 626, 816, 1355-56, 1403, 1439, 1473, 1505-06, 1591, 1616

Wishing

625-26, 634, 703, 972

Additional Health Themes

65, 264, 553, 564, 636, 835, 870, 884-85, 1160, 1175, 1219, 1270, 1316, 1493, 1552, 1570, 1624

HOLIDAYS AND BIRTHDAYS

April Fools' Day

769, 1595

Bastille Day

200

Birthday

214, 217, 219, 384, 391, 404, 418, 421, 647, 704, 861, 1054, 1059, 1158, 1163, 1228, 1439, 1441, 1445

Chinese New Year

403

INSECTS

Ant

9, 237, 575, 696, 756, 944, 1036

Bee

38, 44, 60, 244, 248, 449, 468, 667, 696, 777, 919, 941, 971, 1007, 1208, 1311, 1535

Butterfly and Caterpillar

61, 79, 80-81, 367-68, 513, 696, 753, 756, 765, 1008, 1089, 1109, 1204, 1434, 1589

Additional Insects

25, 246, 523-24, 586, 608, 653, 692, 735, 756, 776, 801, 1005, 1020, 1243, 1283, 1295, 1601

LANGUAGE RHYMES

Arabic

471, 1004

Chinese

925, 1038, 1471

Dioula

1036

French

11, 98, 420, 732, 798, 856, 881, 1021, 1255

German

1001

Countdown Plays Beginning with Ten

Countdown Plays Beginning with Two

Counting

Counting Plays Beginning with Five

Counting Plays Beginning with Ten

Counting Plays Beginning with Two

Counting Out

Animal Sounds

37, 146, 201, 213, 226-27, 229, 234, 244, 252-54, 285, 293, 296, 298, 305, 312, 325-26, 341, 370, 374, 386, 413, 455, 463, 468, 498, 547, 558, 563, 570, 600, 611, 631, 638, 651, 654, 688, 728-29, 761, 775, 798, 802, 812, 836, 851, 859, 886, 919, 924, 941, 964, 975, 1019, 1029, 1034-35, 1044, 1164, 1168, 1212, 1220, 1231-32, 1274, 1295, 1303, 1375, 1381, 1394-95, 1397, 1400, 1406, 1410, 1424, 1451, 1480, 1545, 1549, 1558, 1568, 1572

Earth and Sky

47, 110-11, 160-61, 282, 365, 687, 690, 776, 997, 1071, 1359, 1449, 1540, 1570

Field or Meadow

597, 752, 986, 1031, 1279, 1524

Mountain

35, 597, 818, 854, 1154, 1391

Night Sky

14-15, 41, 144, 216, 298, 390, 553, 597, 621, 687, 690, 725, 818, 878, 976, 984, 1031, 1034, 1056, 1088, 1456, 1546

Plants and Seeds

76, 119, 121, 134-35, 142, 187, 207-08, 279, 299, 319-20, 332, 355, 428, 437, 453, 462, 490, 540, 549, 567, 591, 603, 627, 640, 645, 656, 665, 679, 684, 689, 691, 778, 789, 807, 894, 909, 913, 946, 1053, 1188, 1206, 1248, 1259, 1264, 1279, 1329, 1359, 1364, 1516, 1532

Sea and Seashore

83, 132, 261, 304, 318, 366, 469, 476, 542, 544, 629, 682, 906, 954, 1127-28, 1294, 1337, 1514

Shadow

273, 597, 1157

OPPOSITES

Index to Fingerplays

In and Out

12, 149, 566, 680, 878, 1111, 1209, 1280, 1318, 1333, 1583, 1623

Left and Right

16, 19, 24, 57, 62, 108, 232, 285, 413, 457, 495, 508, 525, 691, 742, 793, 841, 888, 929, 1035, 1055-56, 1091, 1093-94, 1157, 1199, 1218, 1244, 1262, 1317, 1332, 1365, 1460, 1474-75, 1556, 1609, 1623, 1626

Narrow and Wide

1315, 1317, 1334

Open and Shut

332, 591, 614, 683, 1025, 1210, 1315, 1470, 1476

Up and Down

2, 12, 23, 46, 104-06, 113, 121, 136, 149, 168, 171, 176-77, 183, 185, 193, 263, 266, 373, 388, 399, 409, 431, 433, 451, 483, 491, 496, 507-08, 617-18, 633, 650, 652, 710, 741-42, 744, 747, 752, 758, 780, 797, 804, 806-07, 815, 822, 857, 878-79, 882, 892, 955, 959, 987, 1025, 1055, 1092, 1111, 1146, 1194, 1209, 1221, 1227, 1236, 1251, 1274-75, 1280, 1298, 1315, 1317, 1334, 1337, 1359, 1416, 1449, 1493-94, 1497-99, 1509, 1515, 1525, 1527, 1532, 1542-43, 1579, 1583, 1600, 1602

Additional Opposites Themes

49, 149, 158, 266, 839, 960, 997, 1041, 1130, 1137, 1162, 1187, 1233, 1292, 1337, 1416, 1463, 1467

See also: Size under *Concepts* and **Learning Skills**

RELIGIOUS RHYMES

40, 42, 86, 92, 107, 131, 156, 167, 172-73, 216, 235, 240, 247, 250, 358, 376-77, 453, 470, 475, 506, 532, 657, 687, 721, 766, 768, 819, 828-29, 850, 898, 901, 932, 1129, 1207, 1219, 1268, 1338, 1355, 1378, 1416, 1455, 1483, 1511, 1563, 1620

SEASONS

Fall

21-23, 287-88, 346, 367-68, 410, 454, 491, 686, 736, 738-41, 791, 794-95, 824, 848, 926, 1202, 1272, 1279, 1297, 1422, 1434, 1546, 1567, 1579

Spring

79-81, 157, 190, 201, 242, 321, 332, 356, 367-68, 410, 437, 439, 457, 462, 524, 528, 540, 567, 627, 640, 648, 686, 689, 691, 789, 831, 903, 909, 992, 1184, 1188, 1206, 1248, 1279, 1364, 1599

Summer

33, 201, 410, 439, 597, 684, 686, 756, 776, 997, 1516, 1624

Winter

79-81, 95, 129, 206, 321-23, 369, 410, 437, 439, 489, 524, 527-28, 534, 598, 623, 686, 696, 699, 713, 757, 791, 821, 831, 897, 917, 922, 947, 983, 1030, 1047, 1104-06, 1108, 1123, 1170, 1177-79, 1184, 1194, 1196, 1248, 1250, 1272, 1297, 1318, 1349, 1364, 1366-67, 1430, 1434, 1440, 1516-17, 1520, 1547, 1551, 1561-62

STRUCTURES AND TOOLS

Bridge

815, 987, 1360

Door or Steps

614, 1210, 1499, 1628

Flag

195, 262, 350

Machine

136, 193, 258, 451, 495, 660, 703, 1100, 1186, 1197, 1487, 1621, 1628

Index to Fingerplays

Store or Building

66, 78, 98, 120, 147, 167, 199, 211, 220, 224, 233, 243, 249, 300, 346, 408, 414, 444-46, 449, 456, 470, 477, 492, 624, 631, 670, 683, 750, 733, 776, 808, 818, 830, 879, 900, 910, 932, 1084, 1143, 1209, 1280, 1309, 1330-31, 1338, 1345-46, 1349, 1355-56, 1389, 1442, 1458, 1476, 1530, 1580

Tool

31, 74, 78, 142, 406-07, 629, 644, 726, 864, 913, 1045, 1065-66, 1345, 1361, 1518

Additional Structures

171, 179, 192, 212, 425, 429, 536, 664, 1309, 1484, 1492, 1613

TOYS

Ball

29, 56, 395, 414, 435, 484-86, 536, 604, 703, 767, 873, 1326

Balloon

421, 434, 456, 548, 557, 1319, 1369

Doll

314, 352, 456, 477, 559, 658, 675, 826, 835, 867

Jack-in-the-Box

209, 477, 714-17, 1320

Kite

51, 282, 1416, 1599

Teddy Bear

36, 218, 331, 768, 970, 977, 1115, 1159, 1213-15

1067, 1072, 1081-83, 1085, 1171, 1184, 1187, 1201, 1206, 1248, 1257, 1279, 1326, 1329, 1359, 1366, 1449, 1600

Rainbow
365, 1071

Snow
686, 757, 821, 831, 1047, 1105, 1108, 1123, 1168, 1177-79, 1184, 1194, 1196, 1318, 1366-67, 1434, 1517, 1547

Sun
47, 111, 119, 134-35, 171, 187, 207, 263, 365, 424, 428, 453, 603, 627, 684, 686, 689-90, 778, 789, 821, 828, 831, 933, 1031, 1033, 1053, 1089, 1105, 1157, 1206, 1257, 1279, 1318, 1329, 1359, 1367, 1516, 1570, 1624

Thunderstorm
50, 52, 578, 700, 760, 1052, 1613

Wind
22, 51, 66, 111, 262, 288, 307, 345, 454, 597, 679, 686, 691, 739, 750, 828, 878-79, 947, 1101, 1188, 1248, 1264, 1266, 1405, 1434, 1516, 1539, 1547, 1594-95, 1599

ADDITIONAL SUBJECTS

Book
590, 759, 1326

Candle
172-73, 214, 219, 968, 1059, 1148, 1163, 1228, 1441, 1457

Circus or Carnival
33, 96-97, 193, 223, 373, 378, 1092, 1216, 1281, 1571, 1578, 1607

Index to Fingerplays

Fairy or Giant

143, 320, 443, 685, 696, 803, 934, 1034, 1039, 1125-26, 1233, 1337, 1341, 1386, 1489, 1517

Hunting

58, 70-71, 275, 330, 518, 781, 979, 1013, 1079, 1218, 1220, 1224-25, 1232, 1263, 1279, 1291, 1402, 1465

Indian

276-78, 301, 693, 723, 980, 987, 1244-47, 1289, 1310, 1438

Mail

151, 289, 1016, 1058, 1365

Pirate

957

Ring

1577

Scarecrow

929, 1132, 1546

Smoke

400, 1331

Snowman

95, 206, 32, 369, 527, 534, 598, 623, 821, 897, 917, 947, 983, 1047, 1104-06, 1108, 1196, 1520

ALPHABETICAL BY SUBJECT

The numbers accompanying each individual subject entry below refer you to the corresponding entry number in the Main Index.

Addition

185, 202, 226, 286, 301, 316, 324, 342, 362, 378, 490, 503, 837, 858, 949, 968, 973, 1012, 1221, 1256, 1265, 1424, 1457, 1466, 1478, 1482

Airplane

2, 550, 632, 764, 818, 1411, 1485, 1494, 1553

Alligator or Crocodile

6, 296, 502, 817, 975, 1153

Animal

3, 77, 273, 275, 366, 378, 403, 474, 518, 639, 668, 681-82, 810, 818, 975, 991, 1010, 1073, 1080, 1089, 1114, 1133, 1157, 1168, 1216, 1363, 1393, 1415, 1433, 1488, 1544, 1617

Animal Home

79, 80-81, 137, 185, 190, 201, 211, 241, 273, 367-68, 386, 438-39, 449, 459, 464, 468, 504, 572, 602, 616, 635, 653, 696, 720, 776, 779-80, 804, 808-09, 855, 941, 944, 1073, 1075, 1079, 1109, 1157, 1194, 1212, 1272, 1285, 1297, 1311, 1314, 1322, 1333, 1358, 1433-34, 1488, 1495, 1524

Animal Sounds

37, 146, 201, 213, 226-27, 229, 234, 244, 252-54, 285, 293, 296, 298, 305,

Index to Fingerplays

Ant

Apple Tree

April Fools' Day

Arabic Language Rhyme

Astronaut

Australia

Baby

Back and Forth

Ball

29, 56, 395, 414, 435, 484-86, 536, 604, 703, 767, 873, 1326

Balloon

421, 434, 456, 548, 557, 1319, 1369

Bastille Day

200

Bear

17, 35, 58, 248, 275, 304, 439, 613, 638, 651, 669, 752, 758, 777, 1168, 1376, 1390

Bee

38, 44, 60, 244, 248, 449, 468, 667, 696, 777, 919, 941, 971, 1007, 1208, 1311, 1535

Bedtime Rhyme

15, 39, 67, 82, 107, 117-18, 124, 221, 238, 331, 372, 447, 460, 474, 502, 504, 508, 519, 532, 635, 676, 705, 726, 768, 782, 862, 871, 886, 898, 901, 1019, 1094, 1126, 1204, 1213 14, 1290, 1307, 1312, 1315, 1378, 1389, 1416, 1517, 1521, 1527, 1547, 1564, 1566, 1610

Bell

11, 91, 167, 239-40, 340, 397, 417, 932, 1095, 1097

Bicycle

1023, 1411, 1486

Bird

40, 48-49, 75, 82, 159, 190, 211, 241, 319, 372, 429, 452, 459, 473-74, 508, 547, 572, 586, 597, 602, 606, 634-35, 639, 696, 740, 756, 783, 802, 943, 958,

Index to Fingerplays

972, 1089, 1204, 1208, 1212, 1224, 1238, 1288, 1304, 1311, 1377, 1452, 1462, 1467, 1484, 1495, 1524, 1533, 1536, 1539, 1581, 1613

Birthday

214, 217, 219, 384, 391, 404, 418, 421, 647, 704, 801, 1054, 1059, 1150, 1163, 1228, 1439, 1441, 1445

Blackbird

83, 360, 1162, 1292, 1463-64

Boat

40, 115, 260, 469, 476, 832, 1118, 1127, 1185, 1289, 1337, 1360, 1411, 1553

Book

590, 759, 1326

Brazil

891

Bread

30, 32, 59, 120, 147, 186-87, 224, 249, 301, 488, 505, 511, 749, 830, 910, 1162, 1169, 1622

Bridge

815, 987, 1360

Bus

357, 1542

Butterfly and Caterpillar

61, 79, 80-81, 367-68, 513, 696, 753, 756, 765, 1008, 1089, 1109, 1204, 1434, 1589

Candle

172-73, 214, 219, 968, 1059, 1148, 1163, 1228, 1441, 1457

Car

18, 20, 69, 103, 550, 707, 751, 818, 880, 1026, 1058, 1121, 1335, 1411, 1548, 1553, 1600

Career

18, 32-33, 87, 148, 294, 475, 477, 584, 759, 829, 1027, 1058, 1147, 1195, 1252, 1287, 1357, 1518, 1559, 1580, 1612

Carpenter

74, 78, 1121, 1361

Cat

43, 82-84, 112, 122-23, 146, 190, 215, 283-85, 291-93, 311-12, 375, 446, 448, 450, 463, 469, 533, 561, 563, 570, 586, 613, 639, 674, 688, 728-29, 799, 806, 812, 858, 877, 955, 958, 964, 967, 973, 981, 1018, 1181-83, 1276, 1284, 1312, 1326, 1346, 1375, 1401, 1426, 1480, 1541, 1558

Chickadee

245, 1229, 1417

Chicken

72, 117, 188, 226, 246, 386, 420, 463, 478-80, 504, 515, 547, 558, 570, 617, 638, 688, 851, 924, 964, 1019, 1044, 1122, 1154, 1380-81, 1452, 1466, 1543

Chile

891, 1120, 1382

China

403, 888, 925, 1038, 1411, 1627

Index to Fingerplays

1061, 1081, 1151, 1171, 1219, 1230, 1260, 1286, 1372, 1440, 1551, 1592, 1621

Clown

96, 128, 204, 626, 1383, 1586, 1607

Cobbler

3, 113, 114, 125, 401, 520, 1121, 1293, 1559

Colombia

1147, 1408

Color

10, 21, 137, 141, 156, 163, 233, 255, 287, 290, 323, 398, 421, 500, 738, 795, 820, 824, 848, 930, 933, 1071, 1084, 1089-90, 1139, 1206, 1271, 1305, 1422, 1502, 1506, 1574, 1583, 1592

Columbus Day

115

Concept

178, 664, 1512, 1521, 1547, 1562, 1565

Copy Cat Rhyme

4, 8, 75, 99, 100-01, 133, 382, 389, 410, 797, 882, 888, 914, 1100, 1103, 1508, 1534, 1584, 1593

Costa Rica

8

Costume

130, 375, 499, 649, 1528

Index to Fingerplays

Countdown

Countdown Plays Beginning with Five

Countdown Plays Beginning with Ten

Countdown Plays Beginning with Two

Counting

Counting Plays Beginning with Five

Counting Plays

1216, 1218-21, 1223-25, 1231-33, 1235-42, 1244-53, 1255-58, 1261-63, 1265-67

Counting Plays Beginning with Two

1457-62, 1464-68, 1470-86

Counting Out

38, 170, 354, 364, 733, 758, 996, 1014, 1024

Cow

146, 188, 414, 463, 467, 547, 586, 688, 771, 802, 905, 924, 964, 1384, 1406, 1424

Craft

419, 582, 702, 860, 883, 1176, 1287, 1325, 1357, 1371, 1374, 1489, 1596, 1598-99

Crow

341, 929, 964, 1075, 1279, 1414

Daisy

597, 988, 1140, 1206, 1301

Day and Night

185, 332, 390, 427, 635, 654, 690, 1031, 1033, 1296, 1349, 1378, 1389, 1458, 1563, 1568, 1603

Dessert

32, 94, 120, 219, 243, 391, 404, 418, 531, 695, 704, 749, 792, 844, 861, 869, 1037, 1059, 1103, 1158, 1162-63, 1228, 1287, 1336, 1340, 1439, 1441, 1531, 1587, 1591, 1616, 1625

Index to Fingerplays

Dinosaur
227, 893, 962

Dioula Language Rhyme
1036

Directions
49, 820, 1258, 1315, 1511

Division
816, 1046

Doctor
636, 835, 870, 884, 1559

Dog
73, 75, 146, 285, 309-10, 378, 448, 556, 558, 570, 586, 639, 651, 688, 743, 784, 802, 812, 866, 955, 958, 964, 981, 1029, 1070, 1114, 1168, 1274, 1278, 1314, 1346, 1385, 1400, 1480

Doll
314, 352, 456, 477, 559, 658, 675, 826, 835, 867

Door or Steps
614, 1210, 1499, 1628

Dressing
85, 271, 411, 538, 669, 677, 757, 892, 1270, 1389, 1552, 1570, 1603

Duck

75, 146, 251-54, 412, 513, 547, 558, 570, 613, 631, 654, 688, 836, 924, 1164-65, 1220, 1231-32, 1295, 1452, 1468, 1509, 1545

Earth and Sky

47, 110-11, 160-61, 282, 365, 687, 690, 776, 997, 1071, 1359, 1449, 1540, 1570

Easter

92, 162-69, 225, 242, 255-56, 610, 678, 932-33, 1068, 1078, 1203, 1305, 1469

Ecuador

891

Eggs

166, 226, 255, 471, 515, 517, 933, 1068, 1305, 1382

Egypt

471, 817, 1004, 1153

Elephant

17, 77, 175-77, 234, 257, 378, 433, 530, 639, 651, 956, 975, 991, 1093, 1216, 1363, 1533, 1607

England

388, 815, 1014

Fairy or Giant

143, 320, 443, 685, 696, 803, 934, 1034, 1039, 1125-26, 1233, 1337, 1341, 1386, 1489, 1517

Index to Fingerplays

Fall

Family

Farmer

Fast and Slow

Feelings

Field or Meadow

Finger Rhyme

Fire Engine

259, 1237

Fire Fighter

199, 259, 1237

Fish

75, 211, 260-61, 362, 379, 476, 575, 583, 776, 786, 790, 817, 865, 1009, 1168, 1204, 1238-39, 1271, 1533, 1554, 1629

Flag

195, 262, 350

Flower

80, 111, 119, 167, 263, 332, 353, 356, 437, 457, 462, 490, 597, 603, 627, 640, 684, 755, 776, 778, 789, 827, 992, 1051, 1053, 1089, 1140, 1295, 1359, 1364, 1366

Following Commands

57, 409, 900, 1025, 1107, 1156, 1211, 1447, 1623

Food

30, 94, 120, 133, 165, 236, 247, 301-02, 402, 418, 467, 487, 497, 546, 581, 659, 704, 719, 734, 749, 754, 756, 796, 845, 893, 918, 935, 940, 951, 1005, 1041, 1046, 1060, 1064, 1117, 1154, 1160, 1167, 1198, 1203, 1217, 1370, 1389, 1437, 1444, 1446, 1504, 1529, 1552, 1571, 1581, 1591, 1616, 1629

Fourth of July

53-54, 350, 361, 643, 1491

France

59, 200, 1574

Index to Fingerplays

French Language Rhyme

Friendship

Frog or Toad

Fruit

Game

German Language Rhyme

Ghost or Goblin

Giraffe

Goose

Grandparents

389, 391-93, 423, 571, 622, 734, 1304, 1316, 1350, 1436-37, 1550

Grandparents Day

392

Ground-hog Day

273, 1157

Growing Up

231, 355, 599, 622, 672, 990, 1342-43, 1350, 1453, 1536, 1560, 1565

Guessing Rhyme

184, 402, 436, 500, 534, 579, 602, 616, 1059, 1073, 1075, 1093, 1501, 1540-41, 1582-83, 1586-88

Halloween

43, 112, 126, 130, 184, 210, 215, 268-70, 272, 280,306-08, 338, 348, 363, 375, 405, 450, 499, 509, 526, 533, 588, 641, 649, 655, 663, 701, 706, 709, 813, 869, 907, 926, 934-35, 937, 946, 984, 1034, 1069, 1088, 1132, 1135, 1138, 1190, 1242, 1254, 1313, 1336, 1399, 1425, 1507, 1519, 1521-22, 1528, 1538, 1541, 1546, 1549, 1603-05

Hand Rhyme

11, 77, 98-102, 409, 529, 535, 568, 573, 680, 748, 873, 927, 1025, 1086, 1107, 1110-11, 1151, 1191, 1223, 1317, 1332, 1362, 1407, 1444, 1460, 1462, 1474-75, 1498, 1510, 1512, 1592, 1608-09, 1626

Hanukkah

156, 172-73, 250, 968, 1207

Index to Fingerplays

Jack-o-Lantern

126, 184, 210, 280, 509, 526, 588, 701, 706, 907, 937, 946, 1138, 1190, 1313, 1519, 1522, 1538, 1541

Japanese Language Rhyme

183, 822, 895-96

Kangaroo

64, 639, 727, 991, 1124

Kitchen Utensils or Dishes

139, 425, 487, 536, 661, 912, 1005, 1060, 1064, 1222, 1340, 1611, 1627

Kite

51, 282, 1416, 1599

Kwanzaa

1148

Left and Right

16, 19, 24, 57, 62, 108, 232, 285, 413, 457, 495, 508, 525, 691, 742, 793, 841, 888, 929, 1035, 1055-56, 1091, 1093-94, 1157, 1199, 1218, 1244, 1262, 1317, 1332, 1365, 1460, 1474-75, 1556, 1609, 1623, 1626

Lion

17, 378, 651, 761, 991, 1216

Machine

136, 193, 258, 451, 495, 660, 703, 1100, 1186, 1197, 1487, 1621, 1628

Index to Fingerplays

Months and Days

Mother Goose Rhyme

Mother's Day

Mountain

Mouse

Musical Instrument

Narrow and Wide

Nature

Night Sky

Open and Shut

332, 591, 614, 683, 1025, 1210, 1315, 1470, 1476

Opposites

49, 149, 158, 266, 839, 960, 997, 1041, 1130, 1137, 1162, 1187, 1233, 1292, 1337, 1416, 1463, 1467

Owl

298, 413, 450, 474, 498, 774, 838, 1034-35, 1452, 1549

Panama

1446

Pancakes

28, 351, 697, 843

Pat-a-Cake Rhyme

28, 72, 387, 399, 414, 734, 833-34, 954, 995, 1024, 1036-38, 1041, 1128, 1619

Peace

235, 350, 403, 1040

Peek-a-Boo Rhyme

26, 48, 484, 895, 962, 969, 1042-43, 1151

Penguin

991, 994, 1250

Peru

891

Quiet Time Rhyme

21, 75, 99-100, 108, 197, 383, 529, 573, 615, 633, 635, 693, 708, 747-48, 755, 823, 841, 875, 902, 1022, 1034, 1100, 1155, 1183, 1191, 1233, 1242, 1246, 1299, 1312, 1358, 1458, 1472, 1533

Rabbit

67, 70, 75, 95, 118, 123, 185, 189, 313, 378, 430, 433, 438, 447, 449, 464, 570, 607, 609, 613, 639, 756, 776, 779, 781, 801, 803, 814, 862, 881, 887, 908, 927, 942, 945, 958, 1029, 1077, 1079-80, 1098, 1120, 1142, 1183, 1225-27, 1256, 1273, 1277, 1282, 1306, 1311, 1379, 1402, 1454, 1465, 1533

Rabbit (Easter)

162-65, 168-69, 225, 242, 256, 610, 678, 933, 1078, 1305, 1469

Rain

47, 69, 111, 135, 157, 171, 187, 207, 263, 353, 365, 424, 453, 593, 603, 627, 684, 686-87, 689, 702, 778, 789, 828, 890, 916, 939, 997, 1050-51, 1053, 1067, 1072, 1081-83, 1085, 1171, 1184, 1187, 1201, 1206, 1248, 1257, 1279, 1326, 1329, 1359, 1366, 1449, 1600

Rainbow

365, 1071

Reindeer (Santa's)

93, 174, 315, 466, 503, 630, 904, 1012, 1496

Religious Rhyme

40, 42, 86, 92, 107, 131, 156, 167, 172-73, 216, 235, 240, 247, 250, 358, 376-77, 453, 470, 475, 506, 532, 657, 687, 721, 766, 768, 819, 828-29, 850, 898, 901, 932, 1129, 1207, 1219, 1268, 1338, 1355, 1378, 1416, 1455, 1483, 1511, 1563, 1620

Remembering

585, 923, 1061

Index to Fingerplays

Ring
1577

Robin
201, 316, 449, 634, 804-06, 1099, 1364, 1452, 1544

Rocket Ship
14, 144, 232, 694, 725

Rose
98, 119, 134, 591, 628, 1113

Russia
826

Russian Language Rhyme
28, 734, 772, 814, 1581

Safety Rule
5, 16, 105, 109, 141, 510, 751, 782, 793, 1026, 1057-58, 1090-91, 1159, 1199, 1200, 1202, 1274, 1426, 1448, 1485, 1556, 1569, 1624

Sailor
115, 317, 921, 1128, 1223, 1258

Samoan Language Rhyme
416, 1101

Santa Claus
93, 150, 174, 315, 440-41, 466, 503, 630, 685, 698, 863, 904, 1012, 1131, 1481, 1496, 1564, 1585

Scarecrow

929, 1132, 1546

Scotland

829, 1347, 1427

Sea and Seashore

83, 132, 261, 304, 318, 366, 469, 476, 542, 544, 629, 682, 906, 954, 1127-28, 1294, 1337, 1514

Senses

16, 37, 45, 62, 181-83, 313, 426-27, 438, 464, 473, 544, 560, 565, 569, 576, 578-79, 593-94, 596, 651, 763, 777, 785, 800, 823, 868, 885, 896, 936, 990, 1032, 1064, 1076, 1142-43, 1242, 1291, 1308, 1327, 1339, 1365, 1375, 1461, 1470-71, 1501-02, 1513, 1544, 1560-61, 1567, 1595, 1610

Shadow

273, 597, 1157

Shape

59, 110, 152-55, 160-61, 183, 488, 497, 505, 713, 816, 876, 931, 1104, 1143

Sharing

106, 235, 290, 392, 421, 487, 531, 604, 626, 816, 1355-56, 1403, 1439, 1473, 1505-06, 1591, 1616

Sheep

146, 463, 504, 547, 688, 770-71, 802, 812, 964, 1348-49, 1357, 1374, 1582

Shoes and Boots

39, 55, 113, 114, 125, 203, 401, 411, 418, 422, 520, 538, 587, 648, 757, 873, 930, 939, 998, 1081, 1171, 1270, 1293, 1440, 1502

Index to Fingerplays

Size

32, 34, 40, 45-46, 54-55, 74, 114, 119, 143, 175-79, 192, 204, 238, 252, 317, 356, 395, 397, 401, 434, 443, 459, 465, 485, 491, 551-52, 557, 629, 653, 660, 721, 767, 821, 825, 839, 912, 915, 917, 952, 1047, 1093, 1104, 1106, 1134, 1136-37, 1164-65, 1177, 1185, 1190, 1196, 1275, 1281, 1289, 1302, 1323-24, 1343, 1350-52, 1383, 1443, 1452, 1459, 1461, 1468, 1500, 1523, 1550, 1617

Skunk

616, 1089, 1629

Smoke

400, 1331

Snail

638, 808, 1166, 1172, 1174, 1322

Snake

149, 159, 433, 474, 611, 666, 1295, 1363

Snow

686, 757, 821, 831, 1047, 1105, 1108, 1123, 1168, 1177-79, 1184, 1194, 1196, 1318, 1366-67, 1434, 1517, 1547

Snowman

95, 206, 321-23, 369, 527, 534, 598, 623, 821, 897, 917, 947, 983, 1047, 1104-06, 1108, 1196, 1520

Soldier

19, 145, 324, 1011, 1261-62

Spain

387, 555

Spanish Language

387, 891, 1008, 1120, 1139, 1147, 1382, 1408

Rhyme

1446, 1608

Sparrow

325-26, 776, 780

Spelling Rhyme

72, 215, 905, 1014, 1278

Spider

171, 474, 575, 586, 653, 796, 956, 1341

Sports or Hobbies

5, 62, 129, 286, 489, 541, 668, 906, 938, 1117, 1160, 1168, 1177, 1521, 1554, 1615

Spring

79-81, 157, 190, 201, 242, 321, 332, 356, 367-68, 410, 437, 439, 457, 462, 524, 528, 540, 567, 627, 640, 648, 686, 689, 691, 789, 831, 903, 909, 992, 1184, 1188, 1206, 1248, 1279, 1364, 1366, 1599

Squirrel

328-30, 394, 665, 696, 744, 756, 791, 809, 1013, 1194, 1263, 1272, 1291, 1297, 1358, 1366, 1403, 1579

St. Patrick's Day

279, 320, 398, 1039, 1259

Index to Fingerplays

Store or Building

Structure

Subtraction

Summer

Sun

Teddy Bear

Telling Time

Thanksgiving

Thunderstorm

Tickling Rhyme

181, 415, 420, 448, 471, 478, 480, 731-32, 919, 925, 1036, 1096, 1115-16, 1141, 1172, 1174, 1321, 1581, 1589

Tiger

758, 975, 991, 1404

Tool

31, 74, 78, 142, 406-07, 629, 644, 726, 864, 913, 1045, 1065-66, 1345, 1361, 1518

Top

456, 477, 529, 568, 1597

Touching Rhyme

26, 63, 100, 116, 128, 181-82, 184, 231, 393, 408-09, 414-16, 426-27, 430, 433, 478-80, 537, 539, 574, 576, 596, 601, 618-19, 650, 671-72, 709, 719, 730-31, 785, 822, 875, 885, 896, 902, 920, 936, 990, 1074, 1076, 1081, 1087, 1094, 1096, 1104, 1112-14, 1156, 1213, 1315, 1327, 1339, 1447, 1461, 1470-71, 1481, 1490

Toy

431, 456, 492, 662, 856, 1144, 1193, 1255, 1479

Toy Soldier

349, 456, 484, 1614

Train

88, 148, 396, 432, 458, 472, 545, 550, 652, 811, 889, 966, 993, 1049, 1308, 1411, 1553

Tree

21-22, 77, 178, 190, 241, 287-88, 298, 342, 353, 355, 360, 452, 459, 528,

Index to Fingerplays

Turkey

Turtle

United States

Up and Down

Uruguay

Valentine's Day

Vegetable

Vehicle

407, 952, 1197

Water Bodies

211, 251-52, 254, 260, 327, 631, 654, 669, 752, 776, 790, 817, 830, 832, 987, 1118, 1153, 1295, 1419

Wind

22, 51, 66, 111, 262, 288, 307, 345, 454, 597, 679, 686, 691, 739, 750, 828, 878-79, 947, 1101, 1188, 1248, 1264, 1266, 1405, 1434, 1516, 1539, 1547, 1594-95, 1599

Winter

79-81, 95, 129, 206, 321-23, 369, 410, 437, 439, 489, 524, 527-28, 534, 598, 623, 686, 696, 699, 712-13, 757, 791, 821, 831, 897, 917, 922, 947, 983, 1030, 1047, 1104-06, 1108, 1123, 1170, 1177-79, 1184, 1194, 1196, 1248, 1250, 1272, 1297, 1318, 1349, 1364, 1366-67, 1430, 1434, 1440, 1516-17, 1520, 1547, 1551, 1561-62

Wishing

625-26, 634, 703, 972

Witch

215, 338, 375, 450, 641, 813, 934, 984, 1088, 1507, 1549, 1603-05

Wren

13, 281, 720

PART
III

SPECIAL
INDEXES

FINGERPLAYS FOR CALENDAR DAYS

This calendar is designed to celebrate special days and events throughout the school year. The asterick (*) symbol marks holidays listed in the subject indexes. For more information about the fingerplays listed in this section, refer to the Main Index.

SEPTEMBER

Back to School Month
So many children, it's going to be fun
This is the circle that is my head
Today was the day for school to begin

Safety Rules
At the curb before I cross
Do you know what traffic lights say to you
I shut the door and locked it tight
Little Jack Horner stood on the corner (crossing street)
Open the car door, climb inside (fasten seat belt)
The police officer stands so tall and straight (crossing street)
Police officers are helpers (crossing street)
Red on top
Red says STOP
Stop on the corner, watch for the light
The traffic policeman holds up his hand (crossing street)
When I walk home from school today (crossing street)

*Grandparents Day.
  Observed the first Sunday after Labor Day.

277

Index to Fingerplays

Autumn Begins
Autumn leaves are falling down
Little leaves fall gently down
Many leaves are falling down
When the leaves are on the ground
Who comes creeping in the night (Jack Frost)

OCTOBER

Adopt-a-Shelter-Dog Month
Five little puppies in a kennel door
A little doggie all brown and black
This little doggie ran away to play
This little puppy said, "Let's go out to play"

National Popcorn Month
I am a popcorn kernel
Popcorn, popping, pop, pop, pop
Pop! Pop! Pop! Pour the corn into the pot
Sing a song of popcorn
Take a little oil
Yellow kernels we will take

2 World Vegetarian Day
Can you plant a cabbage, dear
Chop, chop, choppity-chop
Five little peas in a pea-pod pressed
I eat my peas with honey
I have a special piece of land just outside my door
Let us make a salad bowl
Nice Mister Carrot makes curly hair

3 Child Health Day
After my bath, I try, try, try
First I loosen the mud and dirt
My nose can't smell
There are many things I can do all by myself (health care)
This is the way we wash our hands

9 Fire Prevention Day
Clothes on fire, don't be scared
Such jolly fun to rake the leaves (lighting fires)

The fire station's empty
Five little firefighters sit very still
Ten brave firemen sleeping in a row
When the siren blows

14 National Friendship Day
I have two friends and they have me
Little friend just over the way
My friends are sweetly smiling
Policeman stands so tall and straight
There once was a man who was tall, tall, tall
This is my house, cozy and neat
To see what he could see a little Indian climbed a tree
Two little friends are better than one
You are my friend

20 Ringling Brothers and Barnum and Bailey Circus
Opened in New York City, 1873.
The circus comes to town today
Going to the circus to have a lot of fun
Ten circus wagons, painted oh, so gay

31 *Halloween

NOVEMBER

National American Indian Heritage Month
Five little Indians by the tipi door
Five little Indians on a nice fall day jumped on their ponies and rode
    far away
The Indians are creeping
John Brown had a little Indian
To see what he could see a little Indian climbed a tree
There were five great big Indians
This is a forest of long long ago

17 Homemade Bread Day
The baker's truck comes down the street
Oh, I walked around the corner (bakery shop)
Slice, slice, the bread looks nice
You put some flour in

21 World Hello Day.
Use this fingerplay to say hello in five different languages: Bon Jour

(French), Buenos Dias (Spanish), Guten Tag (German), Bon Giorno (Italian), Marhaba (say Mar ha ba quickly to make one Arabic word), all mean hello.

I say "Hello" to friends at school

*Thanksgiving

DECEMBER

21 Pilgrims landed Plymouth Rock, 1620.
Five little pilgrims fish in the morn
Five little pilgrims on Thanksgiving Day

Winter begins
Old Jack Frost came last night
It bites your toes and nips your nose
Merry little snowflakes falling through the air
Said the first little snowflake
Snowflakes dancing merrily
Snowflakes whirling all around
This is how the snowflakes play about
This is the way the snow comes down upon a winter day
When cold winds blow
When it is winter time
When it's cold, you shiver and you quiver

Winter Safety Rules
Let's go walking in the snow (danger of slipping on snow)
Let's put on our mittens and button up our coats

*Hanukkah
Jewish Festival of Lights. (This festival may be observed in November.)

25 *Christmas

26 *Kwanzaa
African-American family observance in recognition of traditional African harvest festivals. Kwanzaa means "first fruit" in Swahili.

JANUARY

5 Bird Day
Help birds by feeding them during winter and by protecting them all year. Sometimes observed with Arbor Day.
As little Jenny Wren was sitting by her shed
Bird comes
Five little chickadees sitting at the door
Five little owls in an elm tree
Five little sparrows sitting in a row
Go to sleep now, little bird
Here's a wide-eyed owl
I saw a little bird go hop, hop, hop
If I were a bird, I'd like to be a robin to fly
Into their hives the busy bees crawl (birds in winter)
Little brown sparrows flying around
Little canary yellowbreast sat upon a rail
Little red robins flying around
Little Robin Redbreast sat upon a rail
Once I saw a little bird
One little bird with lovely feathers blue sat beside another one
Tap, tap, tap goes the woodpecker
Ten little chickadees sitting on a line
Ten little pigeons sat in a line
Ten little pigeons sitting on a fence
There were two blackbirds sitting on a hill
This little bird flaps its wings
Three little chickadees looking very blue
Two little birds sat on a stone
Two little blackbirds sitting on a hill
When a robin cocks its head

15 Martin Luther King Jr. Day
Civil rights leader was born in Atlanta, Georgia, on this date in 1929. His birthday is observed this month as a national holiday.
Peace is my dream

15 Hat Day
Celebrate the different kinds of hats worn by people around the world. Observed on various January days.
I wear a big and funny hat
My hat, it has three corners
One day as I was riding on the subway

Index to Fingerplays

18 Pooh Day
>*Celebrate the birthday of A. A. Milne, author of Winnie the Pooh, born in*
London, England, 1882.
The bear went over the mountain
Five little cubby bears tumbling on the ground
Here is a cave, inside is a bear
A little brown bear went in search of some honey
This little bear has a soft fur suit
This little honey bear was playing peek-a-boo

*Chinese New Year

FEBRUARY

Afro-American History Month
>*Observe important achievements by Afro-Americans. These fingerplays*
>*have an Afro-American heritage:*
Green Sally up, Green Sally Down; Green Sally bake her possum brown
One-ry, two-ry, dickery seven
This little pig wants some corn

National Children's Dental Health Month
I have a little toothbrush
If I were a dentist, I know what I would do
Up and down, and round and round (brushing teeth)

2 *Groundhog Day

9 National Weather Service established, 1870.
Black clouds are giants hurrying across the field of the sky
Boom, bang, boom, bang
From big black clouds the raindrops fell
I hear thunder
I listen to the raindrops fall
In the sky in daytime light, we can see the sunshine bright
It drizzles, it rains
Lightning bolts shoot from the cloud
Merry little snowflakes falling through the air
Oh! Where do you come from, you little drops of rain
Pitter-pat, pitter-pat, oh so many hours
Pitter, patter falls the rain
Snowflakes whirling all around
Some little raindrops come quietly down
Ten little raindrops dancing on the walk

This little wind blows silver rain
The wind came out to play one day
The wind is full of tricks today

14 *Valentine's Day

MARCH

Art Month
Draw a circle, draw a circle, round as can be
Here's a little yellow
I helped paint a pine cone for Mother
It's a very rainy day (working with scissors)
See. see, see! What colors do I see
Snip, snip snip the paper (making a valentine or another gift)
This is the way we paste our collage

1 National Pig Day
Pigs are one of the most useful and intelligent animals in the world.
The first little pig danced a merry, merry jig
Five little pigs out by the old farm gate
"It's time for my piggies to go to bed," the great big mother piggy said
"Let us go to the wood," said this pig
Piggie Wig and Piggie Wee
Piggy on the railway
This little pig makes an "oink, oink, oink"
This little pig wants some corn
This little pig went to market
This pig got into the barn

3 Doll Festival, Japan
Five little rag dolls sitting up tall
Flop your arms
I have a dear little dolly
My dolly is a lady

8 Joseph Lee
Developer of children's playgrounds, born 1862.
Ride with me on the merry-go-round
See-saw, see-saw, up and down we go
Up a step, and up a step, and up a step, and up
Up the steps we will go

Index to Fingerplays

11 Johnny Appleseed Day
The anniversary of the death of John Chapman, known as Johnny Appleseed, 1847.
Apple green, apple red
Away up high in the apple tree, two red apples smiled at me
Five red apples hanging in a tree
Five red apples in a grocery store
Here are two apple buds growing on a tree
Here is a tree with its leaves so green
Here's a little apple tree
If I were an apple and grew on a tree
Look at my apple
Ten red apples grow on a tree
Ten rosy apples high in a tree
We will carry this basket

14 Casey Jones (John Luther Jones)
American railroad engineer, born 1864.
Choo, choo, choo, the train runs down the track
Down by the station early in the morning
Here comes the choo choo train
Here is an engine
Here is the engine on the track
I go on a train that runs on a track
I'm a big, black engine on a long freight train
A little train stood on the track
One is the engine, shiny and fine
One red engine puffing down the track
This is choo-choo train puffing down the track

17 *St. Patrick's Day

Celebrate Spring
Drip, drop, drip, spring rain has come no doubt
Flowers tall, flowers small
I dig, dig, dig, and I plant some seeds
In spring, the gently falling rain makes the earth all green again
I took a little seed one day
I work in my garden, plant seeds in a row

21 Memory Day
Dedicated to improving memory skills.
Old John Muddlecombe lost his cap
Poor Old Jonathan Bing

25 Pancake Day
Pancakes were first served in a New York restaurant, 1882.
Bake pancakes nicely browned
Flapjacks, flapjacks, hot-on-the-griddle cake
Is everybody ready to make pancakes
Mix a pancake

APRIL

Be Kind to Animals Month
The American Society for the Prevention of Cruelty to Animals was established, 1866.
Call the puppy, give him some milk
The farmer wakes up early and puts on his workday clothes (farm animal care)
Five little farmers woke up with the sun (farm animal care)
Good Mother Hen sits here on her nest (care of chickens)
I had a bird and the bird pleased me (feeding different animals)
I have a kitty cat named Puff
I have five pets
I had a little poodle (animal care)
In the farmyard at the end of the day (farm animal care)
A kitten is hiding under a chair (animal care)
"Little squirrel, living there in the hollow tree (keeping wild animals free)
Let's pretend we're having fun at a picnic everyone (kindness to insects)
My darling little goldfish hasn't any toes
My dog, Duke, knows many tricks
My kitten tries to bat my ball
Once I saw an ant hill (kindness to insects)
Puppy jumps over a stick (playing with pets)
Ten little pigeons sat in a line (feeding birds)
This is Brownie's dog house (animal care)
When the farmer's day is done (farm animal care)

1 *April Fool's Day

2 International Children's Book Day
I like to peek inside a book
Now I'll tell you a story and this story is new
When the sun lights up the sky (story hour)

Two wheels, three wheels on the ground

1 *May Day

1 Mother Goose Day
See Mother Goose Rhymes in the subject indexes.

* Mother's Day
Observed the second Sunday in May.

25 National Missing Children's Day
Five strong policemen standing by a store
I shut the door and locked it tight (don't open door to strangers)
Two little bunnies going hop, hop, hop (beware of strangers, guns)

Memorial Day
Honors Americans who died in wars.
Five little sailors putting out to sea
Five little soldiers standing in a row
Old Davy Jones had one little sailor
One, two, three, four, five in a row
A sailor went to sea, sea, sea
Ten jolly sailor boys dressed in blue
Ten little sailors standing in a row
Ten little soldiers stand up straight
Ten little soldiers standing in a row

JUNE

Adopt-a-Shelter-Cat Month
Five little pussy cats playing near the door
Five little pussy cats; see them play
I have a little kitty
I'm just a lonely little kitten
A kitten is hiding under a chair
Mrs. Pussy, nice and fat, with her kittens four
One kitten with a furry tail
One little, two little, three little kittens
One, two, kittens that mew
One, two, three, four, these little pussy cats came to my door
Softly, softly creeps the pussy cat
This is a pussy, sleek and gray

Index to Fingerplays

This little pussy drinks her milk

Dairy Month
Here is the barn so big, don't you see
This little cow eats grass
This mooly cow switched her tail all day

14 Flag Day
Boom, boom, beat the drum
Five little flags were waving in the breeze
The flag is coming

Father's Day
  Observed the third Sunday in June.
I do the way my Daddy does when we go out to swim
I like to help my dad a lot
When Daddy washes our automobile (helping father)

Summer begins
A little boy (girl) went walking one lovely summer day
You see me in the sky above

Summer Safety Rules
All the children laughing, having lots of fun (life jackets)
Climb up the ladder, hang on to the side
Climbing, climbing up the ladder

JULY

National Hot Dog Month
I'm a little hot dog

14 *Bastille Day

20 Moon Day
  *American astronauts (Neil A. Armstrong and Edwin E. Aldrin Jr.) land
  on the moon, 1969.*
Astronauts blast off in rockets 'way up into space
Do you want to go up with me to the moon
Five, four, three, two, one, zero (astronauts blast off earth)
Inside a rocket ship, just enough room

30 Henry Ford
American car manufacturer, born 1863.
Auto, auto, may I have a ride
I've got a little 'ole pile of tin
My little jalopy is a right good friend
This is our family car

AUGUST

2 National Smile Week
Good day everybody
Good morning, Mr. Sunshine, how are you today
Grandmother, grandfather, do come in
I looked inside my looking glass
My friends are sweetly smiling
Smile when you're happy
Who feels happy, who feels gay

19 National Aviation Day
Observes the birthday of Orville Wright, who with his brother, Wilbur, invented and flew the first airplane in 1903.
The airplane has great big wings
If I had an airplane, zum, zum, zum, I'd fly to Mexico
Little airplane up in the sky, sometimes you're low, sometimes you're high
Two twin airplanes flying high (airplane accident)
Up from the ground with a whir and a roar

26 Krakatoa
A volcano on an Indonesian island erupts, 1883. It was the biggest eruption in history, heard 3,000 miles away.
A mountain beautiful am I

29 Chop Suey
Was prepared and served for the first time in New York City, 1896.
Old man Chang, I've often heard it said
You use the chopsticks

FINGERPLAYS FOR LETTER DAYS

This section is for teachers who assign alphabet letters to days of the year. Letter day words are printed in bold type. Other grammatical forms of these words plus additional letter day words are underlined. For more information about the fingerplays listed in this section, refer to the Main Index.

A

The **airplane** has great big wings
The **alligator** likes to swim
The <u>ants</u> go marching one by one, Hurrah, Hurrah (**ant**)
Apple green, apple red
<u>Astronauts</u> blast off in rockets 'way up into space (**astronaut**)
Auto, auto, may I have a ride
<u>Away</u> up high in the **apple tree**, two red apples smiled at me
Five little <u>ants</u> in an ant hill busily working and never still (**ant**)
Five red <u>apples</u> hanging in a tree (**apple**)
Five red <u>apples</u> in a grocery store (**apple**)
If I had an **airplane**, zum, zum, zum, I'd fly to Mexico
If I were an **apple** and grew on a tree
I'm an **acorn**, small and round
Little **airplane** up in the sky, sometimes you're low, sometimes you're high
Look at my **apple**
Once I saw an **ant** hill
Ten red <u>apples</u> grow on a tree (**apple**)
Ten rosy <u>apples</u> high in a tree (**apple**)
There was one little bird in a little tree (**alone**)
Three little <u>angels</u> all dressed in white tried to get to heaven on the end of a kite (**angel**)
Two twin <u>airplanes</u> flying high (**airplane**)
Up from the ground with a whir and a roar (**airplane**)

291

Way up high in an **apple** tree, one little apple smiled down at me

B

I got to lick the batter **bowl**
I had a little **balloon** that I hugged tight to me
I had a little red **balloon**
I saw a little **bird** go hop, hop, hop
I saw a little **bunny** go hop, hop, hop
I like to peek inside a **book**
I want to lead a **band** with a baton in my hand
If I were a **bird,** I'd sing a song
I'm being swallowed by a **boa constrictor**
I'm bringing home a baby **bumblebee**
In a green and yellow **basket** I found last Easter Day
It's my **birthday**
"Let's go to sleep," the little caterpillars said (**butterfly**)
A little **ball,** a bigger ball, a great big ball you see
A little brown **bear** went in search of some honey
London **Bridge** is falling down
My **birthday cake** is pink and white
Oh, I walked around the corner (**bakery**)
Ohhh—a churning we will go (**butter**)
Old **Bumblebee** came out of the barn
Once I saw a **beehive** out in the maple tree
Once I saw a little **bird**
Once there was a **bunny**
One **bottle** pop, two bottle pop
One little **baby** rocking in a tree
One little **bee** flew and flew
One little **bird** with lovely feathers blue sat beside another one
One! two! three! four! five! I caught a **bee** alive!
One, two, three, four, five, I caught a **butterfly**
1, 2, 3, there's a **bug** on me
One wheel, two wheels on the ground (**bicycle**)
Please, everybody, look at me (**birthday**)
Row, row, row your **boat**
Sift the flour and break an egg (**birthday cake**)
Sing a song of sixpence a pocket full of rye (**blackbird**)
Skim, skim, skim, with the skimmer bright (**butter**)
Slice, slice, the **bread** looks nice
Some boats are big (**boat**)
Sometimes we play with **blocks** like this
Ten green bottles hanging on the wall (**bottle**)
Ten little bunnies all in a row (**bunny**)
There is nothing so sweet as a **bunny**
There was a **bunny** who lived in the wood
There was a little **bunny** who lived in the wood
There were two blackbirds sitting on a hill (**blackbird**)

C

Dashing through the streets in our <u>costumes</u> bright and gay (**costume**)
Draw a **circle**, draw a circle, round as can be
The first little **clown** is fat and gay
Five <u>candles</u> on a birthday **cake**
Five little <u>chickadees</u> sitting at the door (**chickadee**)
Five little <u>chickens</u> by the old barn door (**chicken**)
Five little pussy <u>cats</u> playing near the door (**cat**)
Five little pussy <u>cats</u>; see them play (**cat**)
Five old <u>crows</u> sat by the door (**crow**)
Fuzzy wuzzy **caterpillar** into a <u>corner</u> will <u>creep</u>
Going to the **circus** to have a lot of fun
Guiseppi, the **cobbler** mends my shoes
Here is the **church**. Here is the steeple
Here sits the <u>cock</u> (**chicken**)
Here's a **cup** and here's a cup
I am a **cobbler** and this is what I do
I am making **cookie** dough
I have a kitty **cat** named Puff
I have a little **cuckoo clock**
I hop into the barber's **chair**
I saw a **child** at play today
I touch my nose, I touch my **chin**
I wish I were a <u>circus</u> **clown**
If you spilled flour all over the floor (**cleaning**)
I'm a little **Christmas tree**
Little Arabella Miller found a woolly **caterpillar**
Little **canary** yellowbreast sat upon a rail
A little striped **chipmunk** sat up in a tree
Mix the batter (**cake**)
Mommy put some <u>cornflakes</u> in my favorite bowl (**cornflake**)
Mrs. Pussy, nice and fat, with her kittens four (**cat**)
My little jalopy is a right good friend (**car**)
Nice Mister **Carrot** makes curly hair
Old man Chang, I've often heard it said (**chopstick**)
Once I saw a bunny and a green, green **cabbage** head
Once there were ten little <u>children</u> (**chore**)
One, two, three, four, these little pussy cats came to my door (**cat**)
One, two, three little <u>chickens</u> (**chicken**)
One, two, three, to the woods goes she (**cherry**)
Open the **car** door, <u>climb</u> inside
Pat-a-cake, pat-a-cake, baker's man (**cake**)
Put your finger in the crow's nest (**crow**)
Red is the apple up in the tree (**color**)
Roly-poly **caterpillar** into a room <u>crept</u>
Said the first little **chicken**

D

Dirt comes in colors, black, red, and brown
The <u>dishes</u> need washing (**dish**)
Dreidel, dreidel, dreidel—see the spinning top
Dry **dirt**, wet dirt, oh, what fun
Five enormous <u>dinosaurs</u> letting out a roar (**dinosaur**)
Five little <u>donuts</u> in a bakery shop (**donut**)
Five little <u>dreidels</u> spinning in a row (**dreidel**)
Five little <u>ducks</u> swimming in the lake (**duck**)
Five little <u>ducks</u> that I once knew (**duck**)
Five little <u>ducks</u> went in for a swim (**duck**)
Five little <u>ducks</u> went swimming one <u>day</u> (**duck**)
Five little puppy <u>dogs</u> in a kennel <u>door</u> (**dog**)
Five little rag <u>dolls</u> sitting up tall (**doll**)
Flop your arms (**doll**)
Have you seen the little <u>ducks</u> swimming in the water (**duck**)
Here's a **doughnut** big and fat
Here's the **doughnut**
I **dig,** dig, dig, and I plant some seeds
I have a <u>dear</u> little <u>dolly</u> (**doll**)
I like to help my **dad** a lot
I roll the ball to **Daddy**
I shut the **door** and locked it tight
I think when a little chicken <u>drinks</u> (**drink**)
If I were a **dentist**, I know what I would do
I'm a little **doll** who's been <u>dropped</u> and broken
Let's put on our mittens (**dressing**)
A little doggie all brown and black (**dog**)
Miss Polly had a <u>dolly</u> (**doctor**)
Mummy has scissors, snip, snip, snip (**dress**)
My **dog**, Duke, knows many tricks
My dolly is a lady (**doll**)
My mother (father) said, "It's **doctor** <u>day</u>"
Never go to lunch with a **dinosaur**
Oh, we can play on the big bass **drum**
One friendly **dinosaur** wanted to play peek-a-boo
One o'clock, two o'clock, three o'clock, and four; I found a pretty **daisy** clock close
    by my <u>door</u>
Over the hills and far away (**dream**)
Six little <u>ducks</u> that I once knew (**duck**)
Six little <u>ducks</u> without a shoe (**duck**)
Tap at the **door**

Index to Fingerplays

Ten fuzzy <u>ducklings</u> swimming in the lake (**duckling**)
Ten little <u>ducklings</u>, <u>Dash</u>! Dash! Dash! (**duckling**)
Ten little <u>ducks</u> swimming in the lake (**duck**)
There was a farmer had a **dog**, and Bingo was his name O
There's a little white **duck** sitting in the water
They say that <u>daisies</u> will not tell (**daisy**)
This is Brownie's **dog** house
This little doggie ran away to play (**dog**)
Two little <u>ducks</u> that I once knew (**duck**)
Waddle, waddle, waddle **duck**
When a yellow **duck** walks down the street
You use the chopsticks (**different**)

E

Do your <u>ears</u> hang low (**ear**)
The **earth** is a great big ball
Earth is round
The **Easter** rabbit came one day
The **Easter** Rabbit's helpers, five in a row
An **elephant** goes like this and that
The **elephant** has a great big trunk
The **elephant** has a trunk for a nose
<u>Eyes</u> up (**eye**)
Five **Easter** rabbits standing by the door
Five eggs and five <u>eggs</u>, that makes ten (**egg**)
Five gray <u>elephants</u> marching through a glade (**elephant**))
Five little **Easter** rabbits sitting by the door
Five little elephants rowing toward the shore (**elephant**)
Here are my ears (**ear**)
Here are my eyes, one and two (**eye**)
Here is the **egg**
How many <u>eggs</u> did the hen lay today (**egg**)
I am an **elephant** so big and strong
I had a little **engine**, but it wouldn't go
I have two <u>eyes</u> to see with (**eye**)
Little <u>eyes</u> see pretty things (**eye**)
My <u>eyes</u> can see (**eye**)
On **Easter** day, we go to church
On **Easter** morning the sun comes up
Right foot, left foot, see me go (**elephant**)
Pretend you're an **egg** sunny-side up

Ten little <u>elves</u> dancing in a ring (**elf**)
This little child brought an **egg**
This little **elf** likes to hammer
Turkeys make big ones (**egg**)
Under a toadstool there sat a wee **elf**
Use your <u>ears</u> (**ear**)

F

The **farmer** plants the seeds
Fee, fie, fo, fum, see my **finger**
A **fence** is tall
The **ferris wheel** goes up so high
The **fiddle** sings twiddle, dee, dee
<u>Fingers</u>, fingers, everywhere (**finger**)
<u>Fingers</u>, fingers, <u>flit</u> and <u>fly</u> (**finger**)
<u>Fingers</u> like to wiggle, waggle (**finger**)
The **fire station**'s empty
<u>Fireworks</u> bursting in the night (**firework**)
<u>First</u> the **farmer** plows the ground
<u>First</u> the **farmer** sows his seeds
<u>Five</u> little farmers woke up with the sun (**farmer**)
<u>Five</u> little <u>firefighters</u> sit very still (**firefighter**)
<u>Five</u> little <u>fishes</u> swimming in a pool (**fish**)
<u>Five</u> little <u>fishes</u> were swimming near the shore (**fish**)
<u>Five</u> little <u>flags</u> were waving in the breeze (**flag**)
<u>Five</u> little <u>flowers</u> standing in the sun (**flower**)
<u>Five</u> little <u>frisky</u> **frogs** hopping on the shore (**frog**)
<u>Five</u> little speckled **frogs** sitting on a speckled log (**frog**)
The **flag** is coming
<u>Flapjacks</u>, flapjacks, hot-on-the-griddle cake (**flapjack**)
The **flower** holds up its little cup
<u>Flowers</u> tall, flowers small (**flower**)
<u>Fred</u> had a **fish** bowl
<u>Friends</u>, I have quite a <u>few</u> (**friend**)
Glunk, glunk went the little green **frog** one day
Golden <u>fishes</u> swimming, <u>floating</u> (**fish**)
Here is a froggie, hippety-hop (**frog**)
How many people live at your house (**family**)
I have ten little <u>fingers</u>, and they all belong to me (**finger**)
I have two <u>friends</u> and they have me (**friend**)
I help my **family** by sweeping the <u>floor</u>

299

Index to Fingerplays

This is the mother so kind and good. This is the <u>father</u> who buys our food (**family**)
This is the mother. This is the <u>father</u> (**family**)
This is the way the <u>flowers</u> sleep (**flower**)
Three little <u>frogs</u> asleep in the sun (**frog**)
Three little leopard <u>frogs</u> sitting on a leopard log (**frog**)
To see what he could see a little Indian climbed a tree (**friend**)
Two little eyes that open and close (**face**)
Two little eyes to look around (**face**)
Two little <u>friends</u> are better than one (**friend**)
Two little monkeys **fighting** in bed
When goblins prowl (**fear**)
The whistle blows at the **factory**
Winking, blinking, see that little light (**firefly**)
You are my **friend**

G

Come see my small **garden**, how sweetly they <u>grow</u>
Five little <u>ghosts</u> dressed all in white (**ghost**)
Five little <u>ghosts</u> went haunting on Halloween night (**ghost**)
Five little <u>ghosts</u> went out to play (**ghost**)
Five little <u>girls</u> woke up in their beds (**girl**)
Five little <u>goblins</u> on a Halloween night made a very, very spooky sight (**goblin**)
Five little <u>ground hogs</u> one February day crept out of their dens (**ground hog**)
Friendly <u>ghosts</u> are on their flight (**ghost**)
"**Gobble**, gobble," says the turkey
Grandfather, Grandmother Tat, waved one hand like that
Grandmother, grandfather, do come in
Green, green, green, green
Gum drop, gum drop, in a bowl
Here's a string of wild <u>geese</u> (**goose**)
I work in my **garden**
I'm a bear—hear my **growl**
I'm a friendly **ghost**—almost
I'm **growing**
In my little **garden** bed raked so nicely over
Mr. <u>Gander</u> and Mrs. **Goose** and their <u>goslings</u>, one, two, three, are two and three, which make, you see, a happy family
Mistress Mary, quite contrary (**garden**)
My darling little **goldfish** hasn't any toes

Index to Fingerplays

One little <u>gosling</u>, yellow and new, had a fuzzy brother, and that made two
    (**goose**)
See my pumpkin round and fat (**grin**)
A shy little **ground hog** left his bed
Ten little **gentlemen** standing in a row
Ten little goblins dancing in a ring (**goblin**)
Ten little <u>grasshoppers</u> sitting on a vine (**grasshopper**)
There was a **grasshopper** that was always on the jump
This is my **garden**
We're <u>growing</u> a little **garden** here
The yellow **giraffe** is as tall as can be

H

Bang, bang with your **hammer**
A big black cat with eyes so green went out on the night of **Halloween**
Build a **house** with five bricks
The carpenter's **hammer** goes rap, rap, rap
Clap your <u>hands</u> so gaily (**hand**)
"Come, little children," calls mother **hen**
Five little <u>hearts</u> all in a row (**heart**)
Good Mother **Hen** sits <u>here</u> on her nest
The **hammer** is a useful tool
Hammer, hammer, hammer, I drive the nails so straight
A **hen** sits on a wall
Here's a great big **hill** with snow all over the side
I clap my <u>hands</u> (**hand**)
I have a **head** and eyes that see
I like to ride on a gallopy **horse**
I say, "**Hello**," to my friends
I stretch my fingers away up **high**
I wear a big and funny **hat**
I will make a little **house**
If I were a **horse**—I'd neigh, of course
I'm a little **hot dog**
I'm all made of <u>hinges</u> and everything bends (**hinge**)
I'm going to build a little **house**
I'm gonna pat my little old **head**
I'm **hiding**, I'm hiding
In and out, in and out, now I roll my <u>hands</u> about (**hand**)
Johnny pounds with one **hammer**
Let's build a **house** with bricks

302

Mother **Hen** walks proudly
Mother plays the violin (**horn**)
My **hat**, it has three corners
My little **house** won't stand up straight
Now I will play my little **horn**
Old Dan has two eyes (**horse**)
Old Mr. Pumpkin **hiding** in a box
Old Mister Rabbit had a mighty **habit**
Old Ned had two ears that go flop, flop, flop (**horse**) On **Halloween**, just
   take a peek
One day as I was riding on the subway (**hat**)
One little, two little, three little hunters (**hunter**)
One, two, three, four, five. I caught a **hare** alive
Open, shut them, open, shut them, give them a little clap (**hand**)
Peek-a-boo, peek-a-boo (**hiding**)
Peter hammers with one **hammer**
Pound pound pound pound goes the **hammer**
"Pound, pound, pound," says the little **hammer**
Said this little fairy, "I'm as thirsty as can be" (**hungry**)
She runs for Daddy's slippers (**helper**)
Snip, snip, snip, snippety (**haircut**)
Ten galloping horses galloping through the town (**horse**)
There's a **hole** in the bottom of the sea
This is a nest for Mr. Bluebird (**home**)
This is my little **house**. This is the door
This is the roof of the **house** so good
This little froggie broke his toe (**hurt**)
This little girl does nothing but play (**helpful**)
Two hands have I to hold in sight (**hand**)
Two little hands so clean and bright (**hand**)
Two little hands so soft and white (**hand**)
When I play my little **horn**
Who feels **happy**, who feels gay

I

Five little Indians by the tipi door (**Indian**)
Five little Indians on a nice fall day jumped on their ponies and rode far away
   (**Indian**)
Five little Indians running through a door (**Indian**)
Five little Irishmen all looking for a four-leaf clover (**Irishman**)
Inchworm, inchworm moves so slow

Index to Fingerplays

The Indians are creeping (**Indian**)
John Brown had a little **Indian**
One little, two little, three little Indians (**Indian**)
Ten little **Indian** boys standing in a row
Ten little Indians dancing in a ring (**Indian**)
Ten little Indians standing in a line (**Indian**)
This is a forest of long long ago (**Indian**)
When it is winter time I run up the street (**ice**)

J

First you push him out of sight (**jack-in-the-box**)
First you take a pumpkin (**jack-o-lantern**)
Five little jack-o-lanterns sitting on a gate (**jack-o-lantern**)
Here is **jack rabbit** with nose so funny
I am a pumpkin, big and round (**jack-o-lantern**)
I laugh at my **jack-o-lantern**
I've a **jack-o-lantern**
Jack Frost is a fairy small
Jack Frost paid me a visit
Jack-in-the-box all shut up tight, not a breath of air
Jack-in-the-box all shut up tight. With the cover closed just right
Jack-in-the-box Jack-in-the-Box. Wake up, wake up
Jack-in-the box sits so still
Jelly on my head
Leg over leg (**jump**)
"Little Nose." Where did you get that little red nose (**Jack Frost**)
Old **Jack Frost** came last night
On my **Jack-o-lantern** I will put great eyes
Once there was a pumpkin (**jack-o-lantern**)
This is a very nice **jack-o-lantern**
This is Jack in a box (**jack-in-the-box**)
Three **jelly fish**, three jelly fish, three jelly fish—sitting on a rock
When the leaves are on the ground (**jumping**)

K

Blow, little wind, on my **kite**
The brown **kangaroo** is very funny

Five little <u>kites</u> flying high in the sky (**kite**)
Five little <u>kittens</u> playing on the floor (**kitten**)
Five little <u>kittens</u> sleeping on a chair (**kitten**)
I have a little <u>kitty</u> (**kitten**)
I'm just a lonely little **kitten**
In faraway Australia, across the rolling sea, there lives the small **koala bear** as cuddly as can be
Jump, jump, jump goes the big **kangaroo**
A **kitten** is hiding under a chair
My **kitten** tries to bat my ball
My mother <u>knits</u> my mittens (**knit**)
One **kitten** with a furry tail
One little, two little, three little <u>kittens</u> (**kitten**)
One, two, <u>kittens</u> that mew (**kitten**)
Said the <u>kind</u> **kangaroo**, "What can I do"
The winds of March begin to blow (**kite**)

L

Five <u>little</u> <u>ladies</u> going for a walk (**lady**)
Five <u>little</u> <u>leaves</u> in the autumn breeze tumbled and fluttered from the trees (**leaf**)
Five <u>little</u> <u>leaves</u> so bright and gay were dancing about on a tree one day (**leaf**)
Five <u>little</u> <u>letters</u> <u>lying</u> on a tray (**letter**)
Here's a green **leaf**
I <u>looked</u> in my **looking glass**
I saw a <u>little</u> **ladybug** flying in the air
Ladybug, ladybug, fly away home
Lazy Mary will you get up
The <u>leaves</u> are dropping from the trees (**leaf**)
<u>Leaves</u> are floating softly down (**leaf**)
The <u>leaves</u> are gently falling (**leaf**)
The <u>leaves</u> are green, the nuts are brown (**leaf**)
The **librarian** helps the visitors find
Lightning bolts shoot from the cloud
"A **lion's** knocking on my door"
The <u>little</u> <u>leaves</u> are falling down (**leaf**)
<u>Little</u> <u>leaves</u> fall gently down (**leaf**)
Oh! Here are the <u>little</u> <u>leaves</u> that grow (**leaf**)
Patrick is a **leprechaun**
Step on the corner watch for the **light**
This is the meadow where all the day ten <u>little</u> <u>lambs</u> are all at play (**lamb**)

305

Index to Fingerplays

This is the meadow where all the long day ten <u>little</u> frolicsome <u>lambs</u> are at play
    (**lamb**)
Tonight we're having <u>leftovers</u> (**leftover**)

M

Do you want to go up with <u>me</u> to the **moon**
Five little <u>mice</u> came out to play gathering crumbs along the way (**mouse**)
Five little <u>mice</u> on the pantry floor seeking for bread crumbs or something <u>more</u>
    (**mouse**)
Five little <u>mice</u> on the pantry floor. This little **mouse** peeked behind the door
Five little <u>milkmen</u> got up with the sun (**milkman**)
Five little <u>monkeys</u> jumping on the bed (**monkey**)
Five little <u>monkeys</u> walked along the shore (**monkey**)
Five <u>May baskets</u> waiting by the door (**May basket**)
Grandma **moon**, Grandma moon, you're up too soon
Here is a streamroller (**machine**)
I am a fine **musician**, I practice ev'ry day
I am a fine **musician**, I travel round the world
I had a little **monkey**. He learned to climb a string
I had a little **monkey**. His name was Slimsy Jim
I help my **mother**
I love the <u>mountains</u> (**mountain**)
I **measure** from top of my head to my toes
I'd like to surprise my **mother**, for this is Mother's Day
In a **milkweed** cradle snug and warm
Johnny looked at the <u>moon</u> (**Mars**)
A little **mouse** came out to take a peek
A little **mouse** hid in a hole
Morning comes on quiet feet
A **mountain** beautiful am I
A **mouse** lived in a little hole
The **mule** has two long ears
On Halloween night, five little ghosts went out to have a **marshmallow** roast
One man went to <u>mow</u> (**meadow**)
Pointing left, the waxing **moon**
Ride with me on the **merry-go-round**
Round about, round about, catch a wee **mouse**
See the little mousie creeping up the stair (**mouse**)
See them dance, so! so! (**marionette**)
Slide your fingers into the wide part (**mitten**)
Ten little <u>men</u> standing in a row (**man**)

There's such a tiny little **mouse**
This is little mousie running round and round (**mouse**)
This is the way the postman comes walking down the street (**mail carrier**)
This little **mountain** finds the sun
This little mousie peeped within (**mouse**)
This little **mule** wants corn
Three blind mice (**mouse**)
Three little monkeys jumping on the bed (**monkey**)
Thumbs in the thumb place (**mitten**)
Tick, tick, tick, tick, says the **metronome**
Two little monkeys sitting in a tree (**monkey**)
Up the candlestick he ran (**mouse**)
We went to the **meadow** and what did we see
We'll all be great big monsters (**monster**)
Where are the baby mice (**mouse**)

N

First, a little **nest** in an apple tree
I had a little **nut** tree
I have made a pretty **nest**
I watch the stars come out at **night**
Put your finger on your **nose**
This is a baby ready for a **nap**
This is mother's **needle**
Three little nickels in a pocketbook new (**nickle**)
Up in a tree is a little bird's **nest**

O

Five little owls in an old elm tree (**owl**)
Five oranges growing on a tree (**orange**)
He looks to the left (**owl**)
Here is the **ostrich** straight and tall nodding his head above us all. But when a
  noise he may hear
Here's a wide-eyed **owl**
A little boy went into a barn (**owl**)
Mr. Hushwing sat in a tree (**owl**)
O X

P

Move like this this this, Little puppets, little puppets (**puppet**)
Mrs. Peck **Pigeon** is pecking for bread
My dolly is a lady (**polite**)
My father bought a pumpkin (**pie**)
My **pigeon** house I open wide
My ship sailed from China with a cargo of tea (**present**)
Oh, we skip round the **pot**
On sunny days I go to **play**
One-eyed Jack, the **pirate** chief, was a terrible, fearsome ocean thief
One royal **penguin**, nothing much to do
One, two, policeman blue (**police officer**)
Peace is my dream
Pease **porridge** hot
Peekaboo, I see you
Piggie Wig and Piggie Wee (**pig**)
Piggy on the railway (**pig**)
Police officers are helpers (**police officer**)
Popcorn, popping, pop, pop, pop
Pop! Pop! Pop! Pour the corn into the pot (**popcorn**)
Pumpkin red, **pumpkin** yellow, he's a funny, funny fellow
Puppy jumps over the stick
See all the presents by the Christmas tree (**present**)
Sing a song of **popcorn**
Soft kitty, warm kitty (**purr**)
Some little seeds have parachutes (**parachute**)
Stir the pot of **porridge**
Take a little oil (**popcorn**)
Ten little penguins standing on the ice (**penguin**)
Ten little pigeons sat in a line (**pigeon**)
Ten little ponies in a meadow green (**pony**)
Ten little pumpkins all in a line (**pumpkin**)
Ten little puppets dance in a row (**puppet**)
These five little playmates live here (**play**)
This little **pig** makes an "oink, oink, oink"
This little **pig** wants some corn
This little **pig** went to market
This little **present** goes to Mary
This little **pumpkin** was taken to market
This little **puppy** said, "Let's go out to play"
This **pig** got into the barn
Three little pigeons sitting on a fence (**pigeon**)
Three little pumpkins laying very still (**pumpkin**)
The traffic policeman holds up his hand (**police officer**)
Toot, toot, toot the horns (**party**)
Two little puppets, one on each hand (**puppet**)

Index to Fingerplays

Two mother <u>pigs</u> lived in a <u>pen</u> (**pig**)
We have a **pumpkin**, a big orange pumpkin
We went looking for a **pumpkin**
Yellow kernels we will take (**popcorn**)
You and me, we're gonna be <u>partners</u> (**pal**)

Q

I'm a duck—I **quack, quack, quack**
Make one eye go wink, wink, wink (**quiet**)
My hands upon my head I place (**quiet**)
Shhhh . . . be very **quiet**
When it's cold, you shiver and you **quiver**

R

Drip, drop, drip, spring **rain** has come no doubt
Eight tiny **reindeer** pawing in the snow
A fat bunny **rabbit** with ears so tall
Five, four, three, two, one, zero (**rocket ship**)
Five little <u>rabbits</u> under a log (**rabbit**)
Five little **reindeer** standing in a <u>row</u>
Five little <u>robins</u> lived in a tree (**robin**)
Here's a **robot** big and strong
I have a **red** accordian
I like to pretend that I am a **rose**
I listen to the <u>raindrops</u> fall (**raindrop**)
I saw a little **rabbit** come hop, hop, hop
I saw a **rabbit**; I said, "Hello"
If I were a bird, I'd like to be a **robin** to fly
I'm a little **robot** short and square
Inside a **rocket ship**
A little brown **rabbit** popped out of the ground
Little cabin in the woods (**rabbit**)
Little <u>red</u> robins flying around (**robin**)
Little **Robin** <u>Redbreast</u> sat upon a rail
Little **Robin** <u>Redbreast</u> sat upon a tree
Little white **rabbit** sits wiggling his ears
My little **rabbit** does not have much fun

My **rabbit** has two big ears
Oh, can you make a **rabbit**
Oh! Where do you come from, you little drops of **rain**
Old John Muddlecombe lost his cap (**remember**)
One, two, three, four, five little **reindeer** stand by the gate
Pitter-pat, pitter-pat, oh so many hours (**rain**)
Pitter, patter falls the **rain**
Purple, blue, green, yellow, orange, and <u>red</u>, six colors in a bow overhead
   (**rainbow**)
Rabbit ain't got no tail at all
Rabbit in a hollow sits and sleeps
The **raccoon** tail am <u>ringy round</u>
Rain is falling down
Rain on green grass
<u>Raindrops</u>, raindrops! Falling all around (**raindrop**)
Robin, **Robin**, <u>Redbreast</u> sits on a <u>rail</u>
Robot, **robot**, do as I command
See the little **rabbit** with his big long ears
Some little <u>raindrops</u> come quietly down (**raindrop**)
Ten little bunny <u>rabbits</u> living on a farm (**rabbit**)
Ten little <u>rabbits</u> in a <u>row</u> so even (**rabbit**)
Ten little <u>raindrops</u> dancing on the walk (**raindrop**)
This little **rabbit** said, "Let's play"
Twelve little rabbits in a **rabbit** pen
When a **robin** cocks its head
Where, oh where is my little **ring**

S

At night I <u>see</u> the twinkling <u>stars</u> (**star**)
Bend and <u>stretch</u>, reach for the <u>stars</u> (**star**)
The big round **sun** in an April <u>sky</u> winked at a cloud
A chubby little **snowman** had a carrot nose
Come to the **store** with me
Down in the grass, curled up in a heap lies a big **snake** fast asleep
Down the chimney dear **Santa Claus** crept
Draw a **square**
An eency weency **spider** went up the waterspout
First the body and then the head (**snowman**)

311

Index to Fingerplays

312

Let's make a **sandwich**
Little Bo-Peep has lost her **sheep**
The little brown **seed**, so tiny and <u>small</u>, that was waiting under the ground
"Little brown <u>sparrows</u> flying around (**sparrow**)
The little grey **squirrel** <u>searches</u> around to find the nuts that have fallen down
A little **seed** so <u>soft</u> and round
The little **snail** is in no hurry
"Little **squirrel** living there in the hollow tree
Make a ball of <u>soft</u>, white <u>snow</u> (**snowman**)
Merry little <u>snowflakes</u> falling through the air (**snowflake**)
My Daddy's **saw** <u>sings</u> a funny <u>song</u>
My fingers are so **sleepy**
My friends are <u>sweetly</u> smiling (**smile**)
My nose can't <u>smell</u> (**sick**)
Now I am a **snowman**
Now I'll tell you a **story** and this story is new
Old Davy Jones had one little **sailor**
Oh, you funny, funny **snowman**
The old **scarecrow** is such a funny man
Old shoes, new <u>shoes</u> (**shoe**)
On top of **spaghetti** all covered with cheese
Once there was a **snowman**
One day I went to sea, chop, knee (**sea**)
One little **star** was out last night
One little, two little, three little **snowmen**
One, two, three, four, five in a row (**soldier**)
One, two, three, four, five. Five little <u>squirrels</u> <u>sitting</u> in a tree (**squirrel**)
Over there the **sun** gets up
Pick up some <u>snow</u>; pack it hard and round (**snowman**)
Pot on the <u>stove</u> goes bubble, bubble, s-s-s (**spaghetti**)
Roll a <u>snowball</u> large (**snowman**)
Roll a <u>snowball</u> round and round (**snowman**)
Roll him and roll him until he is big (**snowman**)
Roll the <u>snow</u> over and over (**snowman**)
<u>Said</u> the first little **snowflake**
Sailing in the boat when the tide runs high
A <u>sailor</u> went to sea, sea, sea
Santa Claus will soon be here
Scarecrow, **scarecrow**, turn around
The <u>seals</u> all flap their <u>shining</u> flips (**seal**)
<u>See</u> my big and **scary** eyes
See-saw, **see-saw**, up and down we go
<u>Six</u> little <u>snails</u> lived in a tree (**snail**)
Slowly, <u>slowly</u>, very slowly creeps the garden **snail**

Wind the bobbin up (**sewing**)
You see me in the <u>sky</u> above on a <u>summer's</u> day (**sun**)

T

Black clouds are giants hurrying across the field of the sky (**thunderstorm**)
Boom, bang, boom, bang (**thunderstorm**)
Choo, choo, choo, the **train** runs down the <u>track</u>
Dive, little **tadpole**, one
Do you know what <u>traffic</u> <u>lights</u> say to you (**traffic light**)
Down by the station early in the morning (**train**)
Draw a **triangle**
Elm <u>trees</u> stretch and stretch so wide (**tree**)
Five big <u>turkeys</u> sitting on the gate (**turkey**)
Five brown <u>teddies</u> sitting on a wall (**teddy bear**)
Five Christmas <u>trees</u> in a forest green (**tree**)
Five fat <u>turkeys</u> all gobbling about (**turkey**)
Five fat <u>turkeys</u> are we (**turkey**)
Five fat <u>turkeys</u> were sitting on a fence (**turkey**)
Five little <u>teddy bears</u> on my bedroom floor (**teddy bear**)
Five little <u>tulips</u> bright and gay (**tulip**)
Five little <u>turkeys</u> flew up in a <u>tree</u> (**turkey**)
Five little <u>turkeys</u> standing in a row (**turkey**)
Five little <u>turkeys</u> were standing by a door (**turkey**)
The great big **train** goes up the track
<u>Here are two apple buds growing</u> on a **tree**
Here are **two** <u>telegraph poles</u>
Here comes the choo choo **train**
Here is a **turkey** with his <u>tail</u> spread wide
Here is a window in a **toy shop**
Here is an engine (**train**)
Here is the engine on the <u>track</u> (**train**)
I am a funny hoppity **toad** trying to jump across the road
I am a little **toad** living by the road
I am a <u>tall</u> **tree**
I am a **top** all wound up <u>tight</u>
I go on a **train** that runs on a <u>track</u>
I have a little **toothbrush**
I have a **top**
I have **ten** little fingers, **ten** little <u>toes</u>
I hear **thunder**
I met a **turkey** gobbler when I went out to play

U

Here we go **up**, up, up
My **umbrella** is a little tent
My **uncle** came from Chile
Pray open your **umbrella**
Put <u>up</u> your **umbrella** to keep yourself dry

V

Chop, chop, choppity-chop (**vegetable**)
Five cheerful <u>valentines</u> from the ten-cent store (**valentine**)
Five gay <u>valentines</u> from the ten-cent store (**valentine**)
Five little <u>valentines</u> all in place (**valentine**)
Five little <u>valentines</u> were having a race (**valentine**)
Five pretty <u>valentines</u> with lace galore (**valentine**)
I have a special piece of land just outside my door (**vegetable**)
Jack ran up to Jill's front door (**valentine**)
Mother plays the **violin**
One, two, three, four, five, when will the <u>valentines</u> arrive (**valentine**)
One purple **violet** in our garden grew
This **valentine** is for bobble-dee-boo
To every friend of mine I'll send a pretty **valentine**
A **valentine** for you
Valentines, <u>valentines</u>: red, white, and blue (**valentine**)

W

As little Jenny **Wren** was sitting by the shed
The busy **windshield wiper** goes "A-dash, a-dash, a-dash"
Five little jinny birds hopping by my door (**wren**)
Five little <u>witches</u> on Halloween night (**witch**)
The funny, fat **walrus** sits in the sea
Help me <u>wind</u> my ball of **wool**
Here's a **witch** with a tall, tall hat
I have a little **watch** right here
I put my finger in the **woodpecker**'s hole

Index to Fingerplays

I **wish** I may I wish I might
If I could have a **windmill**
If I were a **witch**, I'd ride on a broom
If your fingers **wiggle**, cross them one by one
I'm digging in my garden to find a fishing **worm**
In Frisco Bay, there lived a **whale**
In my house are windows, two, shining clear and bright (**window**)
It bites your toes and nips your nose (**winter**)
It's fun to look around and see the things that I would like to be (**wishing**)
Jenny Wren last week was wed (**wren**)
A little **witch** in a pointed cap on my door went rap, rap, rap
Mother's washing (**wash**)
My lady Eucalyptus stretches so tall (**wind**)
One little, two little, three little witches (**witch**)
See my fingers walking, **walking**
See the **window** I have here
See-saw! The woodmen work. The woodmen of San Juan (**woodman**)
Slip on your raincoat (**wading**)
Tap, tap, tap goes the **woodpecker**
This is the sheep so white (**wool**)
This is the sun, high up in the sky (**weather**)
This is the white sheep (**wool**)
This little **wind** blows silver rain
A tiny, tiny **worm** wriggled along like this without a sound
Under a stone where the earth was firm (**worm**)
Warm hands, **warm**
The **watch** on my arm makes a little click
"Who's that tickling my back?" said the **wall**
Wiggle, **wiggle**, fingers right up to the sky
The **wind** came out to play one day
The **wind** is full of tricks today
Witch, old **witch**, how do you fly
Witch, **witch**, where do you fly
The **woodpecker** pecked out a little round hole
You can take your dirty clothes and throw them in the tub (**washing machine**)

X
_____

Here is a box (inside the box , place an **x-ray** picture of a tooth or a picture of a
   xylophone)

318

Y

Here is a **yellow** daffodil
Here's little **yellow**
If I'd put a feather in my hat, I'd look like **Yankee Doodle**
"Peep, peep, peep," says the little chicken **yellow**
Row, row a-fishing we'll go (**yummy**)

Z

At the **zoo** we saw a bear
I know a little **zigzag** boy who goes this way and that
If I had an airplane, **zum, zum, zum**, I'd fly to Mexico
My **zipper** suit is bunny brown
One, one, the **zoo** is fun